OPEN
FOR BUSINESS
UNLOCKING YOUR
INNER ENTREPRENEUR

GARY KEESEE

OB1B24
4.24/2

TABLE OF CONTENTS

OPEN FOR BUSINESS

What would she do? What could she do? The consequences were terrifying. She had to get to Elisha. He would know what to do. She ran to find him. Finally, still out of breath, she began to explain to him that when her husband had died, she had debt that they were unable to pay back. The creditor had given notice that they were now going to take her two sons to work off the debt. Would he help her? Elisha's response was a little strange, "How can I help you? What do you have in your house?" "Nothing" she said, "nothing at all except I have just a little bit of oil left!" The prophet's eyes lit up, and he then instructed her to go and gather as many pots as she could. Once they were collected, she was to take the little oil that she had and pour from her pot into the pots that she had borrowed until they all were filled. Then, she was to go and SELL THE OIL, pay off her debts, and live on the rest.

Why didn't the prophet give her money? What was he looking for when he asked her what she had, knowing that she was in great need? The answer to this mystery is life-changing. To put it simply, he was looking for money. Oh, yes, that is what she needed to pay the debt. But where is money found? Only one place—in the marketplace! God's answer to her was a business; she became an oil tycoon. It is so sad to see that good people are still waiting for God to just dump money into their laps from heaven. The fact is, God does not have any money. Every piece of money in the earth today is stamped with an earthly kingdom. Money is not found. It is created by commerce, a function of business.

I asked a group of people about their vision for their lives one day. One said they wanted to start an orphanage in Africa. Another said they wanted to help inner city women. And yet another said they had a vision of feeding the poor. They were all very excited about their visions as they spoke about them. My next question was where the money to fund their visions was coming from. They all just stared at me. Without wavering, all three said God would supply it. I agreed, but then I asked them how God would supply it. They again stared at me; and this time, they said nothing.

Very simply, without nets, you cannot catch fish! Where are your nets? What can God fill to fund your life, your passion, and your assignment? For most people, there is no answer. For decades, the church has made business, money, and profit distasteful. People sat in their churches and patiently waited for money to just show up, and it didn't. Sadly, the church has not been taught how God brings wealth into the hands of the believer, and because of this, the church is weak and broke. Most people believe that we find money. The truth is, we create wealth, not find it. How? Through creative ideas and concepts.

In this book, I share about the poverty mindset that is in the church today, which holds so many back from what God would have for them. Simply put, without money, people are trapped in slavery and a survival attitude toward life. I discovered that unless people first fix the money thing in their lives, they can never discover their destinies. Why? Because it takes money! Through stories of success and examining Kingdom principles, *Open for Business* inspires and helps people posture themselves for success in God's Kingdom.

Note: Chapter one is a review of Kingdom law, how Drenda and I discovered the Kingdom, and how our lives were radically changed. So even if you are familiar with my other books, I would suggest that you still take the time to read all of chapter one as a review.

—Gary Keesee

LOOKING FOR MONEY IN ALL THE WRONG PLACES!!!

I can remember when the call came in like it was yesterday. Oh, it was not the first call I had like this one. No, it was rather normal for that season in my life. It was morning, and the call went something like this.

"Mr. Keesee, this is so and so from XYZ collection agency. I have called you three times about this overdue $1,600, and every time, you told me you would send me the check. But I have not received it. So, I am calling to tell you that you have three days to get me the money, or I will be filing a lawsuit against you for the money that is due my client." Click!

There was no conversation. He did not ask me a question but was very clear. I had three days to get them the money owed them. Wow, $1,600 was a ton of money at the time. Our refrigerator was empty, and I had no real money due to be paid to me anytime soon.

I was in sales at the time and lived exclusively on commissions. Unfortunately, to have commissions coming in, you had to have made a few sales. In my case, I had not done that. In fact, I had been so paralyzed with fear at the time that I did not want to leave my house. I was having serious panic attacks and was on antidepressants. And to tell you the truth, I saw no way out. But I had one thing going for me, which was my family. First of all, Drenda, my wife, in spite of the hell I was dragging her through, still loved me. And I had four (now five) of the best and most beautiful kids in the world. But I was under so much stress at that time that I hardly noticed them.

Drenda and I were Christians at the time and still are. I had graduated from Oral Roberts University in Tulsa with an Old Testament degree and also attended a couple of years of Bible School along the way. We met at ORU and were married while we lived in Tulsa. Although I went to college to someday go into ministry of some sort, when I had completed school, I felt the Lord lead me to work in sales in the financial field for a while. Tulsa's economy was built around the oil business, and when the oil market began to decline, so did Tulsa. Praying about what to do, we both felt the Lord was leading us back to my hometown in Ohio. Starting over there was not easy.

Although I worked hard at getting my financial business up and running, it seemed I was always falling further behind. At the time of the phone call I referenced, we had ten maxed out credit cards, three finance company loans at a 28% interest rate, two car payments for old broken-down cars, plus we owed my parents and her parents tens of thousands of dollars. We owed the IRS thousands of dollars and had a lot of other smaller debts.

At that time, we had rented a small, old 1856 farmhouse. The house was just as it was in the 1800s. Sounds romantic, but with the duct taped windows, constant onslaught of bees, rats, and other undesirable creatures, it was a challenge. We found the carpet for the bedrooms alongside the road in a trash pile. We found the boys' mattresses in a nursing home's discard pile. Everything else was found at garage sales or at Goodwill. Let me just say this, every day was a day of survival. The saddest thing of all was that this way of life lasted for nine years!

> **TO SURVIVE, WE USED DEBT. AND SLOWLY, THE DEBT KEPT CLIMBING UNTIL THERE WAS NO MORE CREDIT AVAILABLE.**

To survive, we used debt. And slowly, the debt kept climbing until there was no more credit available. Even my parents, when I called them, had cut me off. So, when this bill collector called that morning, this was the state of things. When I hung up with him, I knew we were done. There was no more hope. I was tempted to stop kidding myself and just give up. Although I had been praying for years about this situation, I did not understand why God was not helping us get out of this mess. But this morning, the morning of the call, I knew

I had no hope except God. I went upstairs to our little bedroom on the second floor and laid across my bed in tears. I had to have answers; and as evidenced by my track record and situation, I was missing something. My family deserved better than this. As I was pouring out my soul to God, suddenly, I heard His voice. It was not an audible voice, but up out of my spirit, I heard the words of Philippians 4:19:

> **"My God will supply all your needs according to his riches in Christ Jesus."**

I told the Lord that I knew that Scripture, but my needs were not being met! He answered my question immediately, "Yes, but you have never taken the time to learn how My Kingdom operates. In fact, most of my church lives as Israel lived in the Old Testament, enslaved to Pharoah and making bricks. They live a lifestyle of debt and live a lifestyle of financial bondage. I want My people free!"

I quickly ran downstairs, grabbed Drenda, and told her what the Lord had said to me. I repented to her for not seeking God and learning how His Kingdom worked and for getting us into that mess. We joined hands right there and asked God to help us understand what He meant. At that point, we really did not understand what He meant when He said I needed to learn how His Kingdom worked. I began to study the Bible, and God began to speak to me and show me things that I had never heard before. Before I go on and tell you what God taught me, let me say that understanding the Kingdom was like turning a light on in a dark room. For the first time, we found our answer!

"God, what do you mean by Kingdom?"

When God told me that I had never learned how His Kingdom worked, I was confused, to say the least. Kingdom? So, we prayed, "Lord, teach us what you mean by Kingdom!" The first thing I had to learn was what a kingdom was. I think this concept is hard for our western minds to grasp, living with an American mindset of democracy and free expression. God's Kingdom is not a democracy; it is a kingdom with a king. The authority of the king flows down through the kingdom through various government offices, which then bring the will of the king to the citizens of that kingdom. But let's understand that a mob of people by itself is not a kingdom. No, a kingdom is a mob of people that come under the authority and jurisdiction of a king's government and laws. Those laws lay out the king's will for his people. They provide the framework for life in the kingdom and lay out the benefits and duties of all the citizens of the kingdom.

I FINALLY SAW IT. THE KINGDOM OF GOD IS A GOVERNMENT WITH LAWS. AS A CITIZEN LIVING IN THAT KINGDOM AND UNDER THE LAWS OF THAT GOVERNMENT, I HAD LEGAL RIGHTS AND BENEFITS.

Consequently, you are no longer foreigners and strangers, but fellow citizens with God's people and also members of his household.

—Ephesians 2:19

Stop everything! I finally saw it. The Kingdom of God is a government with laws. As a citizen living in that Kingdom and under the laws of that government, I had legal rights and benefits. The laws work for anyone and everyone in that Kingdom. They are not partial to any one person. Laws do not change. We can send people to the moon because someone discovered the laws that govern the physical world. We fly unafraid in planes at 40,000 feet because we discovered the law of lift, which supersedes the law of gravity. We can put lights anywhere in the world that we want to because we understand the laws that govern electricity and lighting. Do you see it? Could it really be that simple? Laws!

I HAD SPENT MOST OF MY LIFE BEGGING GOD TO HELP ME WHEN ALL ALONG I HAD THE ANSWER.

I then became a fervent spiritual scientist looking for clues. I realized that my view of the Kingdom of God was all wrong. I had spent most of my life begging God to help me when all along I had the answer. When I was young, I was taught that no one knows what God will do; after all, He is God. When we prayed, we were taught that God answered prayer four ways: No, yes, wait, or maybe. Wow, that really helped. But as I studied the Kingdom, I found out that God had already established what He has given to us as citizens, no begging required. It was all laid out in the laws of the Kingdom, and I had a legal right to all of it!

> *This is the confidence we have in approaching God: that if we ask anything according to his will, he hears us. And if we know that he hears us—whatever we ask—we know that we have what we asked of him.*
>
> —1 John 5:14–15

Take a close look at that Scripture and think about what it is saying. It is saying that if you ask anything according to the will of God, the laws of the Kingdom, you can be confident that God's answer is YES! This is not what most churches teach. They teach people that no one knows what God will do, that He is the one who brought the disaster, that He is the one who allowed that person to die from a hideous disease. But His will—expressed by the laws of His Kingdom—is clear. God heals! And He has given this legal right to each and every one of the citizens of His Kingdom.

The King's law is clear: God provides, and He heals. As an example, I was part of a big Christian rally a couple of days ago, and the evangelist was preaching about healing and encouraging the people to receive healing from God. He then went on to tell how his wife died of cancer. His next sentence was, "But God is faithful," and he went on to tell how he met a woman whose husband had also died of cancer, they were married, and how faithful God was in restoring their family. Now, in most Christian circles, this is a perfectly normal story of how God works. However, it is not what the Bible says. Now, do not get me wrong. I am thrilled that God restored his family, but he missed something here. The Bible says,

> *Is anyone among you sick? Let them call the elders of the church to pray over them and anoint them with oil in the name of the Lord. And the prayer offered in faith will make the sick person well; the Lord will raise them up. If they have sinned, they will be forgiven.*
>
> —James 5:14–15

The evangelist said, "But God is faithful" in reference to his family being restored but not in regard to God keeping His Word regarding healing? How can God not fulfill His Word yet be faithful? He can't. He is always faithful!

As we began to learn how the Kingdom worked, our lives were completely changed. The Kingdom impacted every aspect of our family. Let me give you an example.

My daughter Amy, the oldest of my five, had a huge tumor growing in her abdomen. The tumor had been growing for a couple of years, and it was causing her great difficulty. She had severe pain and digestive and urinary tract issues. She had just been married and did not want surgery as she may have lost the ability to have children, and her heart was always to have a large family. So, she did not pursue that option but instead spent time studying what God said about healing until she was totally convinced that healing was God's will for her. She then asked her mother and me to lay our hands on her for healing. Nothing happened at the moment we prayed, but two weeks later, she went to bed and woke completely healed. The pictures you see are eight hours apart! There has been no Photoshop work done on them. She said she did not feel anything throughout the night, but she went to bed like the picture on the left and woke up like the picture on the right.

THE DIFFERENCE OF 8 HOURS!

BEFORE AND AFTER:
13 POUNDS AND 9 INCHES GONE!

She lost 13 pounds and 9 inches in her waist, and her back, which had been knotted and twisted, was completely rebuilt and became normal as she slept. She was healed, no chemotherapy and no surgery!

BEFORE
Spine is straight, intestines are displaced, mass in abdomen

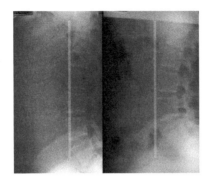

AFTER
Spine is curved, intestines are in place, mass is gone

My daughter-in-law had a tumor the size of a grapefruit in her abdomen and was told it was cancer and she had two months to live. Same thing. She was healed as she slept, with the tumor completely disappearing overnight, no chemo, no surgery, just the Word of God.

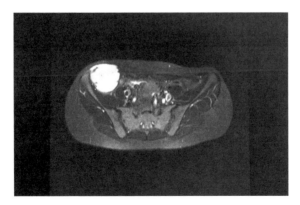

Do not get me wrong. I am not against doctors or anything that helps us get well, but rather I am proving a point. The Bible does not change; God's laws do not change.

"So, Gary, why does it seem that God does not do what He says He will do at times?" Great question, and I will give you a very brief answer here. My other books go into greater detail about this, but let's take a brief look at this question. "But Gary, this book is supposed to be about business." Correct!

<u>But how can you run a business without knowing the laws that will govern the success of that business?</u>

Give me at least this first chapter to lay out some Kingdom basics.

Let's look at a story out of the Bible.

> When they came to the crowd, a man approached Jesus and knelt before him. "Lord, have mercy on my son," he said. "He has seizures and is suffering greatly. He often falls into the fire or into the water. I brought him to your disciples, but they could not heal him."
>
> "You <u>unbelieving and perverse</u> generation," Jesus replied, "how long shall I stay with you? How long shall I put up with you? Bring the boy here to me." Jesus rebuked the demon, and it came out of the boy, <u>and he was healed at that moment</u>.
>
> Then the disciples came to Jesus in private and asked, "Why couldn't we drive it out?"
>
> He replied, "Because you have so little faith. Truly I tell you, if you have faith as small as a mustard seed, you can say to this mountain, 'Move from here to there,' and it will move. Nothing will be impossible for you."
>
> —Matthew 17:14–20

Okay, here is a story asking the same question that so many ask, "What went wrong?" I would like to point out that just a few chapters earlier, Jesus had already given His disciples authority to cast out demons (Matthew 10). This is why they asked, "Why couldn't we cast it out?"

So, what was the reason the demon did not leave? Well, Jesus tells us, "You unbelieving and perverse generation." **Perverse is calling good bad and something bad good. So,** in this case, assuming that God allowed the demon to stay in the boy and accepting that outcome when Jesus had clearly given them the authority to cast out demons would be considered perverse. The demon should have come out! Jesus clearly told them the reason the demon did not come out. He did not say it was God's will the demon stay there and torment that child. No, He proved that when He took over, kicked the demon out, and it left immediately. But Jesus said unbelief was the reason, not that God changed His mind. They were not in faith, thus heaven had no legal jurisdiction to make the demon leave. I know that what I have just said may seem strange to you.

So, let me ask you this, Did Jesus ever face a situation where He could not heal? Probably most people would answer that question with a no.

Take a look at Mark 6:1–2 and Mark 6:4–6.

> *Jesus left there and went to his hometown, accompanied by his disciples. When the Sabbath came, he began to teach in the synagogue, and many who heard him were amazed.*

Jesus said to them, "A prophet is not without honor except in his own town, among his relatives and in his own home." **He could not do any miracles there***, except lay his hands on a few sick people and heal them. He was amazed* **at their lack of faith***.*

That's right, Jesus could not heal them because they did not have faith. I think everyone would agree that Jesus had the ability to heal, but in this case, He did not have the jurisdiction to bring healing. He said they did not have faith. So, what is faith? Faith is simply being fully persuaded that what heaven says is true. (Again, trying to make a long story short here. I have included an appendix at the back of the book concerning faith that you need to read.)

You made them [speaking of Adam and Eve] a little lower than the angels; you crowned them with glory and honor and put everything under their feet. In putting everything under them, God left nothing that is not subject to them.

—Hebrews 2:7–8a

When Adam was placed on the earth, God gave him total legal jurisdiction over the earth. He was to rule over the earth on behalf of the Kingdom of God. The text implies that he was crowned with glory and honor. He probably did not wear an actual metal crown, but the analogy shows how Adam was to rule. He had the glory, the anointing of God to rule, and he had the authority to rule, the honor. Just like a government backs up a king's words, so would God back up Adam's words. But, of course, we all know that Adam lost his position of authority over Satan and actually rebelled against God's Kingdom. When Adam rebelled, he lost his place in the Kingdom of God and gave his authority over to Satan. Essentially, Adam kicked God out of his life. The earth then came under the kingdom of darkness. Death, poverty, and sickness took over the earth, and men and women would then live separated from God. We see God's beloved creation now living in the shadow of death (Psalm 23) and ruled by fear.

There was still hope but only if God could find a man who had not sinned and who would willingly give his life in Adam's place. Only then could mankind be set free. But, of course, there was one small problem with that plan. There was no man who was innocent. All of Adam's lineage had been tainted by sin. But God had a plan to bring Jesus Christ into the world, whose life was sinless, yet He was willing to die in Adam's place. Jesus was born from a different bloodline than Adam. Thus, He qualified to pay Adam's price.

God needed someone on the earth to work through to put His plan in place. That man's name was Abram, later to be named Abraham. Abraham believed God when God promised him a son, even though he and Sarah could not have children as they were well past childbearing years. Through Abram's faith, God was able to make a legally binding covenant, essentially a contract with him, which gave God the door He was looking for. It was through this legal door, through Abraham and his lineage, that Jesus came and paid Adam's debt.

However, each person, man, woman, or child, must personally ratify what Jesus has done by calling on the name of Jesus in faith.

And everyone who calls on the name of the Lord will be saved.
—Acts 2:21

When a person calls on the name of Jesus, they are translated out of Satan's jurisdiction and the kingdom of darkness into the Kingdom of God. The Bible calls this being born again. Then, being a part of God's Kingdom, we must learn how that Kingdom operates and all the laws and benefits of that Kingdom. This is just like if I dropped you from an airplane into a new country, you would have to learn how that kingdom functions.

> **WHEN A PERSON CALLS ON THE NAME OF JESUS, THEY ARE TRANSLATED OUT OF SATAN'S JURISDICTION AND THE KINGDOM OF DARKNESS INTO THE KINGDOM OF GOD.**

But I want to go back to that jurisdiction issue. So, let's ask a question here. Why did Satan have to deceive Adam and Eve into rebelling against God? Why couldn't he just demand and take authority in the earth realm? Because Adam had that spiritual jurisdiction and that authority.

He had to go through Adam, the door.

Although Jesus defeated Satan on the cross, mankind is still separated from God, unless they call on the name of Jesus. But mankind still holds the legal claim to live on the earth, as God had given it to them to rule (Genesis 1). This is true whether a person is born again or not. People still own the legal right to live on the earth. I am not saying that they own the rock, the planet. No, God owns that. But when it comes to the affairs of men on the earth, men and woman are in charge. So today, if Satan wants influence on the earth, he has to work through its legal inhabitants, people.

If God wants influence in the earth realm, He must work through people as well. So, God has to work through people, but He has to have legal jurisdiction to do so first. That jurisdiction is made legal when a man or woman stands in agreement with what God says. That is called faith—being fully persuaded of what God says.

I hope this helps you understand what happened in Mark 6. Jesus could not heal there, because although He had the power to heal, there was no faith, no legal agreement between heaven and the earth realm giving heaven jurisdiction in that situation. I know this is a very short explanation, but it is vital that you understand this, which is why, again, <u>I have put an appendix on the topic of faith at the back of this book</u>. This appendix will help you understand more about how the Kingdom works and what faith is. You will learn why faith is required before heaven can move, how we get faith, and how to know if you are in faith. <u>All are requirements to be a successful business person</u>.

What I am trying to do in this first chapter is to lay out a basic understanding of how the Kingdom works and some of the laws that govern it. As you are going to find out in this book, just because you happen to hang your shingle out and open a business does not guarantee you success. In fact, most businesses fail in the first few years of being open. "According to the U.S. Bureau of Labor Statistics, approximately 20% of new businesses fail during the first two years of being open, 45% during the first five years, and 65% during the first 10 years. Only 25% of new businesses make it to 15 years or more."[1]

---

1 Michael T. Deane, "Top 6 Reasons Why New Businesses Fail," Investopedia.com, December 30, 2022

To avoid becoming one of those statistics, we need to be well aware of the laws that we, as business people, have to adhere to, such as zoning, taxes, and more. But there are also laws in the Kingdom of God that we must understand if we are to be successful. Your first takeaway from this book that you must learn is that the Kingdom of God is a government that is governed by laws. We can learn those laws and, through them, do amazing things.

> **THE KINGDOM OF GOD IS A GOVERNMENT THAT IS GOVERNED BY LAWS. WE CAN LEARN THOSE LAWS AND, THROUGH THEM, DO AMAZING THINGS.**

You will need to have total confidence in those laws and the fact that those laws do not change. If circumstances seem to indicate that the laws of the Kingdom have failed, you will need to look for another reason, because the laws of the Kingdom cannot fail.

> *When they came to the crowd, a man approached Jesus and knelt before him. "**Lord, have mercy on my son**," he said. "He has seizures and is suffering greatly. He often falls into the fire or into the water. I brought him to your disciples, but they could not heal him."*
>
> —Matthew 17:14–16

Unfortunately, it seems that most Christians live like the father in our story with the demon-possessed boy. "Jesus, please have mercy on me!" This is how most Christians pray; they beg. They then go into all the reasons why God should hear their case, trying to persuade Him to move on their behalf.

"He has seizures and is suffering greatly. He often falls into the fire or into the water."

By explaining how the boy is suffering, he is trying to play on God's sympathy, making a case that this is serious and deserves His attention. But this is all wrong! Asking for mercy implies that the one you are asking has the power to provide what you need but has not decided to help you. However, as you can see in this story, God had nothing to do with the delay in the boy's freedom. Once the correct understanding of the Kingdom and the will of God were restored in the situation through Jesus, the demon came out immediately. How fast? Immediately!

However, it seems that many, if not most, have judged the Word of God by what they have experienced rather than by knowing God cannot lie and thus immediately knowing there must be another explanation for the Word's apparent failure. The majority of believers assume that since the demon did not come out—and we all know that God has the power to kick demons out, and yet it did not leave—then they must assume that it was God's will that all demons do not come out. The result? We start a doctrine, or a denomination, that teaches that all demons do not come out. But yet there is a very simple reason the demon did not come out. Unbelief!

It is the jurisdiction issue!

Again, understanding spiritual jurisdiction answers so many questions as to why some things happen and why sometimes things do not happen. This issue of jurisdiction will be an important principle to learn as we will be talking about bringing your business under Kingdom jurisdiction a bit later in the book. So, make a few notes now, and we will fill in some details later.

Wow, as Drenda and I began to learn these Kingdom laws and principles, our lives radically changed. We got out of debt in two and a half years, started multiple companies, built and paid for our dream home on 55 acres of some of the prettiest land in Ohio. And the most amazing thing was that we were able to give away hundreds of thousands of dollars, actually millions, to finance and support the Kingdom of God. I would often think, *Am I the same guy that was looking under sofa cushions to find enough change to buy a Happy Meal to split between three children?* Well, I look like the same person, but I have been transformed by what I learned, and you will be too. How all this happened and what God taught me is recorded in my series of five books called, "Your Financial Revolution." (You can get them on Amazon. Just type in Gary Keesee books, and they will pop up, or go to garykeesee.com.)

Become a spiritual scientist! That is what I called myself after God began to teach me the laws of the Kingdom. I would read the Bible with a completely different mindset. I would study each story and look for clues as to how the Kingdom worked. I knew that what I was seeing in each story or event in Jesus's ministry was a Kingdom law or laws operating, and I was desperate to learn them. "How did that happen?" or "Why did something not happen?" were the questions I asked. Every story is written in the Bible to teach you and reveal

> **AS A CITIZEN OF THE KINGDOM, YOU CAN DO THE SAME THINGS THAT JESUS DID. YOU HAVE ACCESS TO THE SAME LAWS.**

to you these Kingdom laws. Hidden behind the shock and awe of the stories you read are Kingdom laws that are yours to use. As a citizen of the Kingdom, you can do the same things that Jesus did. You have access to the same laws.

> *Very truly I tell you, whoever believes in me will do the works I have been doing, and they will do even **greater things** than these, because I am going to the Father.*
>
> —John 14:12

This book will hopefully uncover why so many Christians are not further ahead in life, not just financially but in influence, impact, ministry, and business.

Being Open for Business may just be the answer to all your financial problems and a new beginning for you. I hope so.

WHICH GOVERNMENT?

If you study the history of nations that are impoverished, you're almost always going to find a restrictive and oppressive government system. The government that you live under has a vital role in the freedoms that you enjoy. That's why we should always fight for the freedoms in America.

It's often the case that countries that have had communistic, atheistic governments that deny people the right to be human, the freedom to make choices, don't allow women to be identified as citizens, and don't value human life are the nations that are deeply impoverished. When we were down in Haiti a number of years ago, we spent some time in the capital city. There was no electricity. Trash was piled up because they had no trash collection. Most of the buildings were falling down. In fact, I don't remember seeing a building that was completely intact. In long rows along each side of the roads, there were people lined up with their little tomatoes and the few mangoes they had picked and various other things for sale. It was just pitiful to see their lives. They'd carry dirty drinking water on their heads for miles. It was amazing and very sad to watch what that kind of government does to people's lives.

We also see the same kind of poverty at work around us. I was in a buffet restaurant in Mount Vernon, Ohio not long ago when a lady using a crutch was making her way through the food line. She dropped her plate and just sat down and began to cry. I think our whole table about broke into tears. Go into the dollar store and watch the people that come in. I'm not against dollar stores—we go to the dollar store—but we heard a lady there telling her friend she was going to take a pair of $12 boots back because she found similar boots for $10 down the street. It might take her more than $2 in gas to do that. Having a poverty mentality is penny-pinching, and it comes from fear.

There are issues in Columbus, Ohio, and other large cities, too, but in Knox County, where I live, as of January 17, 2024, 7,440 people of the 58,000 living here make under the poverty level.[2] Being at the poverty level for a family of four is making $2,600 or less a month, and that is before taxes.[3] In my town, Mount Vernon, the county seat for Knox County, 20% of the city's population make less than the poverty level.[4]

---

2 Data USA, datausa.io/profile/geo/knox-county-oh, January 17, 2024
3 "HHS Poverty Guidelines for 2024," ASPE, Office of the Assistant Secretary for Planning and Evaluation, aspe.hhs.gov/topics/poverty-economic-mobility/poverty-guidelines, January 17, 2024
4 2020 census, census.gov

It's just sad to see people in lack like that. What kind of dreams can people have when they are living month to month with nothing left over? Debt becomes a way of life, and fear and hopelessness steal any dreams these people once had. But we know what's doing that to people—the government. Yes, taxes are out of sight, and that is a huge reason people cannot get ahead. But there is a bigger reason.

It's the spiritual government they live under—the kingdom of darkness—that has them in slavery and held hostage to a life that lacks opportunity.

> **IT'S THE SPIRITUAL GOVERNMENT THEY LIVE UNDER— THE KINGDOM OF DARKNESS— THAT HAS THEM IN SLAVERY AND HELD HOSTAGE TO A LIFE THAT LACKS OPPORTUNITY.**

In Genesis, we find that when Adam rebelled, the earth became cursed. Cursed simply implies the absence of God's blessing. Adam, who enjoyed a worry-free life of full provision in the Garden of Eden found himself outside of God's blessing and provision. When God confronted him after his rebellion, God said this to him:

> *"Cursed is the ground because of you; through painful toil you will eat food from it all the days of your life. It will produce thorns and thistles for you, and you will eat the plants of the field. By the sweat of your brow you will eat your food until you return to the ground, since from it you were taken; for dust you are and to dust you will return."*
> —Genesis 3:17b–19

I call this the painful toil and sweat earth curse way of life. All of us were born under the weight of this system. This never-ending pursuit of finding provision overshadows every area of life. Every decision man now makes is filtered through this pursuit. Thus, people are in jobs they do not like, or even hate, just for a paycheck. They have lost all sense of identity and purpose. Man's purpose has now been totally perverted and lost by this quest to find provision.

You might remember being a kid and talking to your best friend and saying, "What do you want to do when you grow up?" The world was the limit, the imagination could take you anywhere. I knew I wanted to be an engineer on the railroad. I had just received a Lionel train set for Christmas, and I loved it. From that moment, I wanted to be an engineer. Of course, I knew nothing about being an engineer. That goal changed many times as I grew up. But you get the point: you could imagine and dream about what you wanted to do and become.

MOST ADULTS DO NOT DREAM AS THEY DID WHEN THEY WERE A CHILD. WHY? BECAUSE THEY FILTER EVERY DREAM THROUGH THE PAINFUL TOIL AND SWEAT EARTH CURSE SYSTEM.

When is the last time you did that? Most adults do not dream as they did when they were a child. Why? Because they filter every dream through the painful toil and sweat earth curse system. Just paying the bills does not offer too much to dream about. People's real dreams have all vanished, and now they just dream of escaping this weight of finding provision by winning the lottery or finding a pot of gold at the end of a rainbow. They dream of five o'clock, the weekends, vacations, and retirement. They dream of survival and having some time to rest. But they are not dreaming like they did as a kid, "What do I want to do?" Being boxed in by debt, with every penny already spoken for, it is no longer a question of what do I want to do, but rather, what do I need to do to pay my bills? Who can I work for that will pay me enough to survive? Let me paraphrase this: I have no options, so let me be a slave.

> *The rich rule over the poor, and the borrower is slave to the lender.*
>
> —Proverbs 22:7

What if I told you that there is a way to restore that dream you had when you were a kid? No, I am not kidding. That is why you picked up this book, right?

Keith was tired of being a slave when he came across my TV broadcast, *Fixing the Money Thing*, a few years ago. He and Kathy, his wife, were glued to the TV as this was the first time they had heard there really was a way out of the rat race. They bought my CDs and books and listened to and read them over and over again. Finally, they began to dream again as God's Word began to change their hopeless mindset.

The first time I met Keith was at one of my Provision Conferences, which I host every year during the last week of April. When we met, he began telling me how he lost his corporate job a few months back but had been listening to my teaching on the Kingdom and how it works for months. He said slowly, his vision for his future began to change, and he realized that he did not want to find another corporate job. He wanted to start his own business. He was convinced that God had a better plan for him than that.

Keith did not really know what he would do as a business, but he did like to work with wood and had some wood sitting around, and thought that he could make and sell furniture. But after trying it for a while, he said he knew that it was not his answer. He also had some background in trucking, so he decided to start a truck hauling business. He had one truck and began to gather a few clients, hauling cars and anything else people needed hauled. He said in his first month, he made just over $4,000 and was thrilled. That was really close to what he had been making in his corporate job, so he knew he was on the right track.

As he kept going with his one truck, he heard through a friend about a company that was looking for more truckers to deliver various commodities they were producing. He decided to check it out. He was excited as he researched the potential he would have driving for this new company. He and Kathy prayed about it and felt they should go in that direction. This would require them to purchase a semitruck, so he did that and began to haul for this company. I can remember Kathy emailing me with excitement not long after that. She said that she had just finished invoicing that new company for over $70,000 for one week's work. As I read it, I just kind of stopped, with a sudden gasp, as I saw that she said $70,000 for that week's work.

They knew they were onto something big. The demand kept getting stronger, so Keith bought two more trucks and hired two drivers. Then, his business was getting more complicated, and he and Kathy realized that they were over their heads in regard to administration and knowing how to run a business. So, they hired a company to come in and train them how to set up their company in regard to processes and administration. The demand kept increasing, so they bought more trucks and hired more drivers. Keith said there were many times that the pressure was tough. He had so much to learn, but Keith and Kathy knew this business was their answer, and they kept learning and growing. This was seven years ago.

Keith now has over 30 trucks on the road in his company and is bringing in over 10 million dollars a year, heading for 20 million. Keith says he has to pinch himself now remembering where he came from and where he is at today. Oh, by the way, he paid cash for all those trucks! His company is debt free, and his life has drastically changed! Is he slowing down? No! He is still buying more trucks and adding more clients almost every month. Keith found out that dreams can still come true.

Kathy said that on the front side of this, they listened to the teaching on the Kingdom every day for two years. They knew that they had so much religious training to unlearn but had no Kingdom training. They knew that they had to completely relearn everything they thought they knew about God and the Kingdom of God.

Keith and Kathy now also travel the country teaching others the Kingdom principles that changed their lives. But Keith and Kathy will tell you that they are not God's special favorites. They know that all of God's children have the same legal rights in the Kingdom that they have. And if anyone will take the time to learn how the Kingdom operates, they can have the same kind of success they have had.

I want to emphasize that it was not Keith and Kathy's great effort and wisdom that is producing millions of dollars a year. If you asked them, they would tell you that absolutely, their success is a direct result of learning the laws of the Kingdom and then applying them.

THEIR SUCCESS IS A DIRECT RESULT OF LEARNING THE LAWS OF THE KINGDOM AND THEN APPLYING THEM.

So, let's dig into this a little deeper. I want to take you to a very famous story in the Bible that most people know but really do not understand, the story of the Prodigal Son. Hang with me here. I know you already know this story, but there is something vital that I must show you and you must understand in this story.

Not long after that, the younger son got together all he had, set off for a distant country and there squandered his wealth in wild living. After he had spent everything, there was a severe famine in that whole country, and he began to be in need. So he went and hired himself out to a citizen of that country, who sent him to his fields to feed pigs. He longed to fill his stomach with the pods that the pigs were eating, but no one gave him anything.

When he came to his senses, he said, "How many of my father's hired servants have food to spare, and here I am starving to death! I will set out and go back to my father and say to him: 'Father, I have sinned against heaven and against you. I am no longer worthy to be called your son; make me like one of your hired servants.'" So he got up and went to his father.

But while he was still a long way off, his father saw him and was filled with compassion for him; he ran to his son, threw his arms around him and kissed him.

The son said to him, "Father, I have sinned against heaven and against you. I am no longer worthy to be called your son."
—Luke 15:13–21

This story is an analogy of Adam back in the beginning leaving Father's (God's) house.

The younger son is Adam in this story, and he is enamored with what he has heard about another kingdom, one that seemed to have so much more potential and excitement than working in the Kingdom of God. He knew Eve was surely for the other kingdom. Of course, we all now know that it was Satan who was filling their minds with these perverse thoughts, insinuating that God was holding out on them, and that he did not have their best interests in mind for them. So, in the story, Adam, the younger son, leaves home, quickly spends all of his money, and is left penniless. A severe famine is in the land, and there is no food. So, in desperation, he does something that he had never done before. He offers to become a slave, a hireling, in exchange for food. Previously, being a son in his father's house, he was waited on by staff, and the food was endless. But of course, he left that life months ago.

> *So he went and hired himself out to a citizen of that country, who sent him to his fields to feed pigs. He longed to fill his stomach with the pods that the pigs were eating, but no one gave him anything.*
>
> —Luke 15:15–16

This son was then doing something that he never would have done back home, feeding pigs. This was a disgrace in the Jewish culture and was considered unclean. But then, he was so desperate that he was willing to exchange hours for dollars, so to speak, painfully toiling and sweating in exchange for survival. Notice that the entire kingdom he was in was in great need. As I said, a severe famine ruled the land, and no one would give him anything. Everyone was out for themselves. So, he became a hireling, a slave, and had completely lost the picture of who he once was.

Now, what I wanted to point out to you is here in this part of the story.

> ***When he came to his senses***, *he said, "How many of my father's hired servants have food to spare, and here I am starving to death! I will set out and go back to my father and say to him: "Father, I have sinned against heaven and against you. I am no longer worthy to be called your son; make me like one of your hired servants." So he got up and went to his father.*
>
> —Luke 15:17–20

In his famished state, he could not help remembering how things were in his father's house, such wealth that even the servants had more than enough. So, he made a plan to go back to his father and say, *"Father, I have sinned against heaven and against you. I am no longer worthy to be called your son; <u>make me like one of your hired servants</u>."*

I want to point out this phrase: he came to his senses! Catch that. This simply means he remembered a picture of how things were back at his father's house.

"Make me like one of your hired hands, a slave," is what the son said to his father when he finally stood before him. But instead of banishing the son to be a slave, the father completely restored him and set him in the estate as a son with full rights and privileges just as if he had never left.

All of us have been trained in this painful toil and sweat system. We know to survive, we must painfully toil and sweat. We equate labor as being the means to provide what we need in life. But I want you to see that in this story, the young man is heading back home, but heading home with a slave mentality, not as a son. A slave mentality was limiting him to survival. Again, he learned that in the other kingdom.

> **ALL OF US HAVE BEEN TRAINED IN THIS PAINFUL TOIL AND SWEAT SYSTEM.**

Now, stop and think about the mentality he had heading home. He felt he was unworthy to be a son. He knew that being a slave would be better than dying of starvation or feeding those awful pigs the rest of his life. So, you can see there were no more dreams there, only a resignation to labor with no means of moving ahead. This is how most people live today! This is how they think. And even though so many are Christians, they are living in Father's house as orphans. This is not because that is what God thinks of them, but rather, it is what they think about themselves.

> **IF YOU DO NOT CHANGE THIS PERCEPTION OF YOURSELF, YOU WILL STAY A SLAVE, EVEN THOUGH GOD HAS PUT HIS ENDLESS RICHES BEFORE YOU AND INVITES YOU TO ENJOY THEM. GOD HAS RECEIVED YOU AS A SON OR DAUGHTER, AND YOU NOW HAVE BEEN GIVEN ACCESS TO THIS INCREDIBLE KINGDOM OF GOD.**

If you do not change this perception of yourself, you will stay a slave, even though God has put His endless riches before you and invites you to enjoy them. God has received you as a son or daughter, and you now have been given access to this incredible Kingdom of God. Pay attention to what God says about you, about the awesome potential you have. Stop agreeing with what people have said about you or even what your parents have said about you. Stop comparing yourself to others. You can do it; you were created to win in life and shine forth the love and power of God to a generation walking in darkness. Again, I could teach you many business principles, but until you learn who you are, who God says you are, and believe it, principles would do you no good.

Okay, so here is my takeaway from the story of the son who left home.

You will never be able to receive from God if you look at yourself as unworthy to receive: if you view yourself as a slave, someone who can't win, someone who does not qualify for the blessings of God. Stop it!!! God is the father in the story who chose to receive that son back, not the other way around. The father, who rejected the thought of his son being a slave, is the same father who greeted him with a kiss and covered him with the finest robe, put the signet ring of authority

> **YOU WILL NEVER BE ABLE TO RECEIVE FROM GOD IF YOU LOOK AT YOURSELF AS UNWORTHY TO RECEIVE.**

back on his finger, and gave him the sandal, representing full access to the estate, as well as the fatted calf, the prosperity of the estate. The son had nothing to do with it; it was all the father's doing.

We all have learned this unworthy and little ol' me attitude from the world, not God. For instance, have you ever offered a gift to someone, and they say, "Oh, I couldn't take that"? Why would they say that? You are the one that is choosing to give it. They had nothing to do with the cost of purchasing the item. You are expressing your will to give them the gift, yet they hesitate. Why? Because they do not feel worthy of receiving the gift. They had done nothing to "deserve it." Or how about this one? You tell your friend that they have a nice dress on, and they reply, "Oh, I bought this down at the Goodwill." Or they might say, "Oh, I bought this on sale down at so and so store."

Why are you ashamed to receive a compliment about what you have and just leave it at that? Why do you feel shame for having a great dress, a great car, or anything for that matter? Because you are afraid that people will talk and say that you are trying to be better than them or you are just showing off. The root of all this is unworthiness. If a king came into the room with exquisite clothing on, no one would expect otherwise. They would think, *He deserves those awesome clothes; he is the king.* Well, who are you?

No, do not be afraid to receive.

Listen, if you disqualify yourself from receiving the promises of God as valid for you, and only see yourself as a loser, then you will never dream big dreams and will always think small and do small things.

Oh, did I say dreams? Yes, I did. Are they important? More than important—essential.

You were given an imagination for a reason. You were created to dream and dream big. Your imagination is not just a foolish waste of time; it is probably the most powerful force needed to move you toward your success.

Let me show you.

> *When tempted, no one should say, "God is tempting me." For God cannot be tempted by evil, nor does he tempt anyone; but each person is tempted when they are dragged away by their own evil desire and enticed. Then, after desire has conceived, it gives birth to sin; and sin, when it is full-grown, gives birth to death.*
>
> —James 1:13–15

Now, James is warning people about what they set their thoughts on. He is stating that thinking the wrong thoughts can bring destruction into your life, taking you down a path that you never intended to go down. That is true, of course. We have seen that happen to many people, and we often wonder how they got this messed up. How did they get here?

In this passage, James gives us insight into how that happens and reveals one of most powerful success principles that has ever existed—how your human spirit and your imagination work to bring things that were not in existence into existence.

James says that when you have a desire, you are tempted or enticed by that desire. Okay, I think we all can relate to that. But how is a desire birthed? Well, you will not have a desire unless it is set before you, something that you have seen or heard. You would never have a desire for an apple unless you saw or heard of one, right? So, for starters, it is very important what you feed on mentally, what you allow yourself to listen to and gaze at.

I was talking to a friend yesterday, and he was telling me about this great movie they were watching last week. They said it was great, but right in the middle of the movie, it went to a scene of this couple making love, with complete nudity. There was no warning. It was a short clip in the movie but enough to birth desire or imagination. Then, he said the rest of the movie was great. Of course, he acknowledged that the movie was rated R, but it was a topic he was really interested in. He assumed that if the movie went that direction, he would just fast forward it past that scene, but he said this scene just appeared with no warning.

I know all of us have gone to a movie and said, "The movie was great, but why did they put that one scene in it?" Well, I can tell you why. It was put there to capture your imagination. This is how marketers work. They know how you were made and can use imagery to capture your imagination. We know, of course, Satan is the one prompting the producers to put that scene in there. He knows how this works, that once you are enticed by that desire and allow it to capture your imagination, the Bible says that the imagination will **drag you** toward the fulfillment of it.

The desire will drag you!

That desire will, if you continue meditating on it, drag you to conceive a plan to fulfill the desire. When the plan is carried out with action, it yields the fruit of that desire. Now, this will work for a negative desire, which is what James is warning us about, but it also works this way for a good desire. You need to understand that your human spirit is designed as an incubator. It will incubate an answer, a plan for whatever you put into it. Again, marketers understand this and work hard to capture your imagination with images. They know once you pick that thought up, that imagination will drag you toward its fulfillment.

I want you to really get a grasp of this concept of being dragged toward success. I know it is hard for many people to drag themselves to work each day. They dread getting up, dread the work itself, and look forward to quitting time. But this is just the complete opposite of that. Being dragged to success by your imagination means that you cannot wait until Monday morning comes around. You love what you do and can't wait to get back at it; it becomes a passion for you. This is what I am talking about. And somehow, we must get your imagination stoked up before we talk about opening a business. The business can't just be about making money; you have to have a passion for it. One of the most well-known success books ever written was *Think and Grow Rich*, by Napoleon Hill. He understood this principle very well. But guess what? He was not the one who invented it. It was in the Bible all along. But let's remember this very important principle:

> Your desire, your imagination will drag you toward its fulfillment.

Now that you understand this, you know why it is so important to allow God's Word to reveal who God is, who you are, and what God says about you. You must renew your mind and thoughts to thoughts that allow you to dream with God.

> *Jesus looked at them and said, "With man this is impossible, but with God **all things are possible.**"*
> —Matthew 19:26

A major key here—with God, all things are possible! Things that were not possible with you are possible with God, so dream big and let God fill your thoughts with His promises.

Dream no small dreams. If your dream is not bigger than the risk, you will fail. Or, let me say it this way. Your dream must be bigger than the problems you will face getting there. This is why Keith and Kathy said they spent the first two years listening to Kingdom teaching every single day. They had to wash out their brain of all

> **THINGS THAT WERE NOT POSSIBLE WITH YOU ARE POSSIBLE WITH GOD, SO DREAM BIG AND LET GOD FILL YOUR THOUGHTS WITH HIS PROMISES.**

the pictures of failure that would stop them when they had to step out of their comfort zone. You cannot allow yourself to feed constantly on the news or media; the news usually only reports bad things. You must think on good things and successful thoughts and allow your spirit to incubate plans of success with God's help.

It grieves me to see people suffering when they do not have to. Religion has taught us so many lies about God. In fact, most Christians will fight you to stay poor. And this grieves me. You know the government of God is not bankrupt. The Kingdom of heaven in you is designed to provide you with every single thing you have need of in life. In fact, the Bible says that you are an ambassador of God.

> *We are therefore Christ's **ambassadors**, as though God were making his appeal through us. We implore you on Christ's behalf: Be reconciled to God.*
> —2 Corinthians 5:20

An ambassador coming to America from Spain or some other country does not pay their own expenses. The government that sent them is responsible for taking care of them. In the same way, your earthly provision is not tied to this earthly bankrupt government system, this kingdom of darkness that we find ourselves in. Our provision comes from a different government—the Kingdom of heaven. The problem is that we, as believers, have not been taught how to navigate this Kingdom of God. Even though we are citizens and have legal rights in this Kingdom, no one has ever taught us how this Kingdom of God works.

OUR PROVISION COMES FROM A DIFFERENT GOVERNMENT— THE KINGDOM OF HEAVEN.

When I teach people that God's Kingdom is a kingdom with laws and a government, most of the time, they have never heard that before. Because of that, very few know how to access what has already been provided for them. Most of the time, Christians are just waiting on God to dispense His mercy, hoping He will hear us and do something for us. Let me just lay out the truth for you. He has done all He can for you. I know what you are thinking, *Well, I do not see much going on in my life. What do you mean He has done all He can for me?*

Legally speaking, you already have everything you need in life and much more. But like here in the earth realm, you could have a trillion dollars in the bank, but unless you went through the legal means to cash a check from that account, you would live in poverty. Most people do not know how to cash the check! Actually, they usually do not even know there is a check, and it already has their name on it.

God wants to prosper you in this land of poverty and stress. He needs you to embrace His goodness and freely receive from Him.

They will be called oaks of righteousness, a planting of the Lord for the <u>display of his splendor</u>.

—Isaiah 61:3b

The "they" in this Scripture is speaking of the church, which you are. Isaiah was prophesying of this day, the church age, where God says that we are going to be like oaks of righteousness. Righteousness is simply what heaven calls right. An oak, of course, is a huge tree that cannot be ignored and is not easily moved. God wants to plant His people all over the earth—in every occupation, in every nation, for one purpose—to be put on display!

That's right, God wants to put you on display. He wants people to see heaven in you. Your display will draw people to the Kingdom of God. They will want what they see you have. I am not talking merely about finances but everything working, everything intact, nothing missing, and peace and joy shining forth from your life.

I have to tell you about this young lady in my church. She came up to me a couple of months ago and told me this amazing story. She is from Brazil, and recently married, but is now living in the United States and is a member of my church. One Sunday in October, I was telling the church one of my hunting stories, how I do not hunt deer but receive them. How I sow a seed and believe God, and they will show up, usually in 30 to 40 minutes. Oh, by the way, when I sow for my deer, I sow for a specific deer. If I want a buck, I sow for a buck. If I sow for a buck over a certain number of antler points, that is what shows up. If I sow for an eight-point buck, that is what shows up. This is one of the ways God taught me about His Kingdom and its laws of operation years ago.

So, in this one service, I asked the congregation, "How many deer hunters do I have in here? Raise your hand." This young woman, her name is Daya, raised her hand. Her husband was shocked. But she was so moved by the examples I was sharing and how the Kingdom works, she said, "Yes, I want to shoot a deer this year." Her husband grew up hunting and had no idea she wanted to hunt. But then she went on. She told her husband that she was not just going to shoot a deer that year, but it was going to be a seven-point buck. Again, he was shocked and asked her why she wanted to shoot a seven-point deer. She said because seven is her favorite number. So, she sowed a seed and prayed over that seed, and she believed that she received that deer the moment they prayed, according to Mark 11:24.

> *Therefore I tell you, whatever you ask for in prayer, believe that you have received it, and it will be yours.*
> —Mark 11:24

So, she kept telling everyone that she was going to shoot a seven-point buck that fall, and they just made fun of her. Let's remember that she had never hunted before, and she was going to be hunting with a crossbow. They would say, "You can't pick what size buck you are going to shoot. It will just be one that comes up to you by chance." But she was unmovable; she was going to shoot a seven-point buck.

So, hunting season finally came, and she went with her husband to land that their family had hunted for years. Ten people were hunting that weekend, all men except her. Again, she made her statement, telling them of the deer she would shoot. And again, they made fun of her. Opening morning, they did not see a thing. She told her husband, "Something is wrong. This stand we are hunting in is not right. Is there not another stand on your property?" Her husband said, "Yes, there is one more, but no one hunts it. It is not a great stand." She said she prayed, and she told her husband that they needed to move to that stand.

The following day, they went out to that stand. Sure enough, a buck showed up, but it was too far for a crossbow shot. But she remembered my stories, and she said that she knew she had the authority to speak to that deer and tell that deer to come closer. She spoke and told that deer to come closer to her, and sure enough, it turned and came into range. She waited for her husband to tell her when to shoot. She took a shot at 35 yards and made a perfect hit on the deer.

As they walked up on the deer, she was so excited, but she was even more excited to see what kind of antlers it had. As she walked

GOD WANTS TO PUT YOU ON DISPLAY. HE WANTS PEOPLE TO SEE HIM IN YOUR LIFE.

up to the deer and counted the number of points it had, she screamed out with joy. It had seven points. She was so excited and could not stop telling everyone about the Kingdom of God. In fact, she went back to Brazil to see her family and told everyone there about her deer and the Kingdom. She told me that 20 people came to Christ there in Brazil because of her story.

God wants to put you on display. He wants people to see Him in your life.

Let me end this chapter with another bit of Scripture that will change how you see yourself.

> *Consider how the wildflowers grow. They do not labor or spin. Yet I tell you, not even Solomon in all his splendor was dressed like one of these. If that is how God clothes the grass of the field, which is here today, and tomorrow is thrown into the fire, **how much more** will he clothe you—you of little faith! And do not set your heart on what you will eat or drink; do not worry about it. For the pagan world runs after all such things, and your Father knows that you need them. But seek his kingdom, and these things will be given to you as well. Do not be afraid, little flock, for your Father has been pleased to give you the kingdom.*
>
> —Luke 12:27–32

If you look at most Bibles, the chapter title for this section of Scripture is: Do Not Worry! First, Jesus says, "consider," meaning stop and contemplate what I am about to say. He says, "Look at the flowers." I am sure you have stopped many times and looked at the flowers. They are amazing, with all kinds of colors and designs. So intricately made. And then there is the scent they give off. They are a wonder of His creation. But then Jesus says something so profound that you just might have missed it, so let me point it out to you.

> *They do not labor or spin.* [My paraphrase: They do not have to painfully toil and sweat—God takes care of them.] *Yet I tell you, not even Solomon in all his splendor was dressed like one of these. If that is how God clothes the grass of the field, which is here today, and tomorrow is thrown into the fire, how much more will he clothe you—you of little faith!*

UNLOCKING YOUR INNER ENTREPRENEUR

Jesus is telling us that not even Solomon in all his splendor was dressed like one of these. Now, you know that Solomon was the richest man that ever lived, right? It is said that he accumulated 1,400 chariots and 12,000 horses. He built a temple and overlaid it with gold. All of King Solomon's goblets were gold, and the Bible says, *"Nothing was made of silver because silver was considered of little value in Solomon's days."*

His wealth was so great that a visiting queen fainted at the sight of all of it!

> *When the queen of Sheba heard about the fame of Solomon and his relationship to the Lord, she came to test Solomon with hard questions. Arriving at Jerusalem with a very great caravan—with camels carrying spices, large quantities of gold, and precious stones—she came to Solomon and talked with him about all that she had on her mind. Solomon answered all her questions; nothing was too hard for the king to explain to her. When the queen of Sheba saw all the wisdom of Solomon and the palace he had built, the food on his table, the seating of his officials, the attending servants in their robes, his cupbearers, and the burnt offerings he made at the temple of the Lord, she was overwhelmed.*
>
> —1 Kings 10:1–5

The actual Hebrew wording here says that there was no more spirit or breath in her. She was shocked beyond words. Some versions say that she fainted. Now remember, she was not broke herself. She came with *"a very great caravan—with camels carrying spices, large quantities of gold, and precious stones."* Yet, she was shocked beyond words. Jesus then says something that should literally cause you to stop and grab your pen, or it could cause you to faint yourself.

Yet, Jesus says, "***How much more*** *will he clothe you—you of little faith*" (Luke 12:28)!

How much more? More than Solomon! Really!

And then if you are not yet overwhelmed, Jesus goes on and says the most incredible statement.

> *"Do not be afraid, little flock, for your Father has been pleased to give you the kingdom."*
> —Luke 12:32

God has been pleased to give us the Kingdom! That means He is giving us legal access to His Kingdom, His wealth, His government. That is far more than Solomon could ever conceive of.

Major Key: You will never reach for the impossible if you think it is impossible!

YOU WILL NEVER REACH FOR THE IMPOSSIBLE IF YOU THINK IT IS IMPOSSIBLE!

A year ago, I needed my car cleaned and waxed. I did not have time to do it, but one of my guys at church told me of a service that came to you and did all that. I had never heard of someone doing that but said, "Yes, schedule them to come out." I was in meetings the day the guy came out, but I was able to step out just as he was finishing up.

The car was spotless. He had personally designed a van with all the equipment in it that would power wash the car, clean everything inside, degrease the engine, wax it—everything was there in this small SUV. I was so impressed with the setup and the results.

So, I asked him, "Did you design all this, or is this a franchise?" He said he had designed and built everything, and it was just him. Now, I was so impressed that I was asking him about the company because I was going to buy stock in it. I thought it was that good. When he said that the business was just him, I asked him, "Are you going to expand this business, because everyone needs this business? Everyone is busy, and this is great." But he said, "No, I have no plans to expand the business. It is just me." I tried to tell him that he was missing out and that he needed to expand and franchise this. But he was not interested.

I knew that someday, he will tire of washing and cleaning cars himself and would need to move the business to a different model, a place where it would produce income without him having to be the one who washed every single car. But he had no interest. I am sorry, but this guy was young with a family. He was missing an opportunity to create a business that could take great care of his family while giving him more time with them, instead of having to be away every minute of the day washing cars.

He is the complete opposite of the guy I sat next to on a plane one day. Although I have mentioned this guy in my other books, it is worth repeating. Sitting next to him, I asked him what he did for a living, and he said he had a bakery. Instantly, I pictured what I had in my town, a small storefront bakery that baked cookies and cakes and did weddings and things like that. So, I asked him how the bakery was doing. His next statement shocked me. He said that he had opened the bakery two years earlier and had done about $20 million in business that year. I think my mouth must have just dropped open. I began to ask a hundred questions to find out how that happened. He said when he launched his business, he launched it to bake for corporations, not to be your small-town bakery. He said when he launched it, he already knew the market he wanted to capture, and he built it accordingly.

HE SAID WHEN HE LAUNCHED IT, HE ALREADY KNEW THE MARKET HE WANTED TO CAPTURE, AND HE BUILT IT ACCORDINGLY.

Let me say that again, "HE BUILT IT ACCORDINGLY!" His dream demanded what he built. Wow!

So, what is your dream?

If you build to survive, that is what you get, survival. So, build to win.

The one guy built the cleaning business to pay his bills. The baker built his business to change his world!

YOU GET WHAT YOU SEE!

As you may know, I am a pastor of a large church, with thousands of people attending. But I have also owned a financial services company for going on 43 years now. We primarily focus on helping people get out of debt and safeguarding their investments. I use many different financial companies in my business, all of them with great products. A few of them also have production incentive trips based on your yearly production.

Well, when I launched Faith Life Church, 29 years ago, I had the number one office for one of my vendors in the entire country out of 5,000 offices. When I launched my church, I knew that it would take a lot of work to get that going, so I assumed that I would not be able to maintain my number one status, which, knowing what I know now, was a dumb assumption. And that is exactly what happened, because I did not know any better than to accept that vision. So then, yes, my production did drop lower after I launched the church. However, I was still very active and was able to maintain about 4- to 5-million dollars in volume with my primary vendor, which was enough to qualify for their annual all expenses paid conference.

Every year at the conference, they would recognize the top producers with a bonus check of $100,000. Although I agreed that it would be great to be able to get a check like that, I saw no way that I could qualify with all I was doing at church. Over the next 18 years, I would do my usual 4- to 5-million dollars' worth of volume and then attend the conference, where I would get to clap for those top people as they got their recognition and check.

But in 2014, as I sat there, the Holy Spirit spoke to me and said, "Why aren't you up there?" I was shocked when I heard that. Of course, I would have loved to be up there, but I had already resigned myself to the fact that it would be impossible to reach the $10 million production level to qualify. After all, I had been working about as hard as I could for the last 18 years and yet maintained my 4-5 million-dollar level of production every year. As I was mulling this around in my head, I heard His voice again, "I want you up there. I want My glory to be seen there." Wow, what could I say?

So, I told Drenda, and we both agreed to sow a seed of faith toward that goal. This conference was in March, so the year was well underway. In the natural, I did not see how to do it. But we sowed our seed, laying our hands on that check and sowing where we felt

God was leading us. We declared and believed that we received $10 million in production for that year.

A couple of weeks after we made that declaration, I had a dream where only three words were spoken, "Seize the moment!" I did not have clarity as to the meaning, but after I woke up and prayed, I understood. As I looked at my processes in the company, when a client called in, we would sometimes be a day in getting back to them. But I felt God was saying that I needed to change how we do things and make sure we call back every client within an hour after they call. The Lord let me know we were losing customers by not getting right back to them.

So, I had all my managers change how they were doing things and made that a policy. We also put a rule in place that from that moment on, any client that was investing over $50,000 with us would have an in-person visit. Now, we are licensed in every state, and traveling to every client would be a big deal. We were previously meeting our long-distance clients over a live computer link, something like Zoom. But I knew that an in-person visit was the very best way to talk to our clients. I mean, who wants to invest a million dollars over the phone? No one! So, we implemented that policy change.

Well, to make a long story short, we ended the year with just over $10 million, and we got the $100,000 check. We had the great privilege of sharing Christ with the audience that day as we went forward to be recognized. We have made that goal in production every year since then, except just missing it during Covid. However, last year, 2023, we did about $34 million, which pushed us way up to being number one in January of 2024. Let me just say this. When I went to the conference in the fall of 2023, there was greater respect from the other leaders and company reps toward me and Drenda than we had ever had before. I was able to share the Gospel with many and give God the glory in that environment.

> **YOU AND GOD CAN DO A WHOLE LOT MORE THAN YOU WOULD EVEN CONSIDER DOING YOURSELF.**

This is what God desires. He loves to raise people up from nothing and make them a gazing stock for His glory. This is what He wants for you too. So again, you and God can do a whole lot more than you would even consider doing yourself.

I mean, for 18 years, I was satisfied with just making the requirements to attend the conference but never thought I could make it to number one. Oh, how that mindset was the problem. It was interesting that I planted a seed (sowed a financial offering) specifically to make it to that 10-million-dollar bonus the first year, and we did just over $10 million by one case. The next year, the company raised the entry production to $12 million, and we did one case over that $12 million level. Are you seeing something here? I was setting the specific amount, and that was specifically the amount that we did. The Kingdom is that specific.

Last year, we sowed to be number one in the company, which we made in January. But an interesting thing happened. The vendor raised the entry production level for the bonus in 2024 to $15 million in production. But, amazingly, we did more than that in the month of January alone. We qualified for the trip and check in one month! Trust me, I never would have thought that was possible. If you are catching on here, you can see that we hovered around that $10- to 12-million mark for a few years. Yes, we made the trips and got the checks. But I knew there was more; we needed to raise our sights a bit. Although we were making the trips and receiving the checks, we were getting lazy again, just like I was during those 18 years. No, I knew I could not settle. I needed to keep going.

I have a friend who owns a really big car dealership. When I met him, his dealership was ranked 90 below the number one spot. I said, "You need to be number one." We agreed with him to do that, and you know what? He eventually did it. He now stands in the top three to five in the nation but is number one in his region. I always say to go for it. Let God build the house. You and God get the glory, and you get the paycheck.

As I said earlier, when Drenda and I began to apply the laws of this Kingdom, our lives completely changed. I mean, really changed. From living in paralyzing fear and poverty to living completely debt free, building our dream home, and being able to give away hundreds of thousands of dollars to promote the Gospel and share this great news of God's Kingdom. I still have to pinch myself every time I think about it. I wish I had time to tell you all the stories and all that Drenda and I have seen. And more than that, what we have seen in other people's lives.

You do not have to be afraid. God's Kingdom is wealthy beyond measure, and He has given it to you! I know, this probably goes against everything you were taught at church, that having money is greedy and not spiritual. But those thoughts are not God's thoughts. He wants you to have it, and He is pleased when you step into it. He knows that there is a dark world out there where people are looking for freedom from the earth curse of poverty and slavery. They need to see hope, and you are it! We are called to be generous!

> *Now he who supplies seed to the sower and bread for food will also supply and increase your store of seed and will enlarge the harvest of your righteousness. You will be enriched in every way **so that you can be generous on every occasion**, and through us your generosity will result in thanksgiving to God.*
> —2 Corinthians 9:10–11

If you are going to be generous on every occasion, then you better have a few bucks sitting around. Because for most people, they struggle just to make their monthly budget, let alone have enough to be generous on every occasion.

Now, before you get bummed out because you are not there yet, just relax. We will start talking about where you are going to find that money in the next chapter.

Drenda and I have evidence in our personal lives that the Kingdom works just like the Bible says it does. We have seen our lives go from being hopelessly in debt and sick to prospering and healthy.

So, after returning from a ministry trip to Albania, when God told me that He was sending me to the nations to share His covenant of financial blessing, we launched our conferences in churches all across the country. I thought everyone would want to know what we found out. I thought everyone would want to know how to prosper, or how to be healed, or how to win in life. But I was wrong.

For instance, a church that had a Sunday morning attendance of 1,200 would have 50 people show up Sunday night to our conference. I thought, *How can this be? They are all broke and in debt. They should be hungry to hear about their freedom.* But this was how it was in almost every church we went to. Usually about one-fourth of their people would show up. I knew something had to change because I knew I had their answer!

When asking many who did not come to the conference why they had not attended, they said that budgets and numbers were boring. They may say that is why they did not come, but I understood the real reason. No one wants to sit there and hear what they should be doing while at the same time realizing how far they are living from that goal. They did not want to look at their finances because they felt like losers and condemned. I can remember those days; I did not like to look at the bill drawer when I had no money to pay the bills.

This grieved me because, sadly, I realized they had given up on winning financially in life. They had now settled for a life of mediocrity and a life of survival. In this state of apathy, people think they are doing all right when they're not. Oh, yes, they have a house to live in, they have their car payment up to date, and their bills are all paid, so they think they're good. But I knew better; I had been there. Living paycheck to paycheck is better than not, of course, but that is not financial freedom.

God's people must wake up. For instance, if I asked someone how they were doing financially, they would say, "Great." Then I would say, "Okay, that is awesome. So, you're out of debt?" Then they would say, "Well, no, but all our bills are paid on time." "Okay, that is good," I would say, but then I would ask them, "How much interest have you given away to the bank this month?"

> *The rich rule over the poor, and the borrower is slave to the lender.*
>
> —Proverbs 22:7

That made them stop and think. People will tell me, "We are out of debt!" "Great, so your house is paid for?" "No, we still have our mortgage, but everyone has a mortgage," they will say. I thought their answer was so strange. Since when was having a mortgage, the most expensive debt people have, not a debt? Look next time at your mortgage statement and see how much of that payment went to the principal and how much went to the bank. I knew that I had to shake things up a bit. I wanted to show people that, yes, it is possible to be completely debt free! Yes, you can win in life. And no, I am not talking about living on a budget so tight that you have to eat peanut butter sandwiches every day just to survive. But on a 30-year loan borrowing $350,000 at 6.5%, only $316 of the $2,212.23 payment is going toward the principal; $1,895.82 is going to the bank. Someone is winning here, and it is not the homeowner.

Now, do not get me wrong. You have to start somewhere; I understand that. And most people will start with a mortgage. And, of course, having a modest mortgage payment is better than having a big rent payment. At least you aren't just paying someone else's mortgage payment with your rent payment. But that is not where it stops. People buy this and that, and before long, they have no options. They are slaves to the lender.

Yes, money is very important, my friend. When I was in serious debt and finally began to seek God for wisdom and understanding concerning how His Kingdom worked, I learned that the average family can be completely debt free, including their mortgage, in less than 7 years without changing their income. But who is telling people that? I know I am. In fact, if you want me to prove it to you, call my office at 1-(888)-397-3328, and we will provide a free, written Get Out of Debt Plan for you and your family. I have been doing that for free for over 30 years. But if you have never heard that you could be free in less than 7 years, you would assume that you would never be free until maybe you were 85 years old. But you see, it is possible; you just need knowledge. Someone has it and is using it against you. Listen, money is important. Don't let your religious friends make you feel that it is not.

I remember getting a letter from someone who saw our broadcast. She was going on and on about how wrong it was that I had this BMW car and such and such. So, I wrote her back and asked her how much she gave to missions last year and how were her own finances. I then told her that I had financed a crusade in Pakistan that year and a hundred thousand got saved. I said to her, "Someone was glad I had some money."

Someone who says, "I'm okay—I don't need any more money," has just revealed they have no concept of the Kingdom and no love for people. Because there is no influence in this realm without money. People have accused me of teaching too much about money, but until we all have too much money, I believe we need to stay on it.

The Kingdom of this earth is run by and leveraged by the need for money. And the lack of money is what keeps people enslaved and in bondage. We have to win in this. It is the most basic challenge to the Christian life, and we have to win that challenge before we can do anything else. Of course, we can lay hands on the sick and they will recover. And we find a lot of sick people out there. But we find so many more people battling this impoverished spirit. So, hang with me through this book. We must break this spirit of poverty, spiritually and mentally. You can be free!

I want to share these verses again.

> *Now he who supplies seed to the sower and bread for food will also supply and increase your store of seed and will enlarge the harvest of your righteousness. You will be enriched in every way so that you can be generous on every occasion, and through us your generosity will result in thanksgiving to God.*
> —2 Corinthians 9:10–11

God is interested in enlarging the harvest in your life so that you can impact people's lives. It's not about the car you drive or the house you live in. Although He will bless you with more than enough if you are all about His Kingdom.

Scripture tells us He wants you to be rich in every way so that you can be generous on every occasion. God wants to demonstrate the riches of His Kingdom in you. Why? Because the other kingdom is bankrupt—and its people are looking for provision. And if God's people can demonstrate that our Father is good and that there is provision in our Father's house, they will come home.

GOD WANTS TO DEMONSTRATE THE RICHES OF HIS KINGDOM IN YOU.

Why do we have an immigration problem between Mexico and the United States?

Money.

There are people in Mexico who are looking for a new government that has more opportunities for them, so they're coming here of their own free will. They're fighting to get in here. They're risking their lives to get here.

I saw an article today that said church attendance is dropping across the United States. You know why? Because religion is boring and condemning. But if Christians were demonstrating the Kingdom, they would be knocking on our doors. Churches would be having an immigration problem. People would be flooding in to be part of what we are doing, just as they flocked around Jesus because He met their needs.

I'm not talking about social programs or potlucks. I'm talking about liberating people from the other government and bringing them into a government of freedom where they have answers.

I told Drenda the other day, "I'm going to start a Bible study in Mount Vernon." She said, "You don't have time." "I don't care," I said. "That's my town. I'm tired of going uptown every day and seeing so many impoverished people there." It just grieves me. I want to go up there and tell them, "You don't have to live like this! There's a way out of your poverty mentality!"

We must win this thing and get it right. I say this all the time, "You will never discover your destiny until you fix the money thing." Oh, you may have a lot of good ideas, but without some money, they are just that, ideas. It is so easy to get messed up with this world's system of thinking. After being trained for 30 years in the wrong Kingdom, it's possible to walk out of a great church service, listen to a newscast for 15 minutes, and then lose your total perspective of the Kingdom of God within you.

I've seen that in myself. More than once, I've listened to an old message that I taught, and I'd think, *Is that me? God, forgive me! I used to believe that strong! I used to walk in this!* We have to keep our minds renewed. It's so easy to get off track.

"You will be enriched in every way…"

"…so that you can be generous on every occasion…"

Which will produce what result?

"…thanksgiving to God."

The people around you will be praising God for their answer! Because someone has some money! And because you are willing to share and help, they will be grateful, they will see the reality of the Kingdom in your life, and they will come home to Father.

> *This service that you perform is not only supplying the needs of the Lord's people but is also overflowing in many expressions of thanks to God.*
>
> —2 Corinthians 9:12

Friend, we can't be ashamed about talking about money! God wants us, and actually needs us, to have money to get stuff done on behalf of His Kingdom.

I remember being invited to a birthday party for a guy in my church. It was held in this great hotel, and there was a room full of people. The dinner was amazing. Later, after we all sang happy birthday to the birthday guy, his wife came over to me and asked me to step over to the corner for a second. She needed to talk to me about something. So, I stepped over to the corner with her, and she said to me, "I don't have any money and no means of paying for this dinner tonight." I said, "Well, just tell them you can bring it in tomorrow." "No," she said, "I can't pay for this dinner tonight or tomorrow or the next day. We do not have any money." I stood there stunned.

Then, her next statement caught my attention, "Could you pay the bill for me?" "Well, how much is the bill?" "$1,800" she said. So, I stood there and said, "That is a lot of money. What were you planning on doing when you knew that you had no money?" She said, "I didn't know, but I felt that with all these people coming, I just could not cancel the party. I knew that you were coming, and I thought that you might help me." And, yes, we did pay the bill that night, and no one but her and her husband knew what had happened. About a year later, they sent me a check for twice the amount I had paid that night. The point is, she knew I had money. There are answers when someone has some money!

Drenda and I were at a big pastors' conference, and I saw another pastor there that I had met a year earlier. He began to introduce me to some other pastors as this was the first time I had come to this conference. But yet the conference was a little strange. No one there except this one pastor I had met a year earlier really paid any attention to Drenda and me. I will admit we felt a little out of place. Everyone was dressed up in their suits, and the atmosphere just seemed religious. Something was wrong. We tried our best to introduce ourselves to people, but there was this weird feeling. It is hard to explain, but we really just felt out of place.

Well, it was the evening dinner break, and my pastor friend asked us to go along with about 20 other pastors that were going to a nearby restaurant. We accepted the invitation. After arriving at the restaurant, we found our way to the table and sat down. The other pastors all came in and also sat down, but still no one spoke to us except maybe the guy I sat next to. The meal was good enough, but I still had this weird feeling, like a wall was up.

After the meal and dessert, the server brought the bill to the table and asked who wanted it. No one said a word, and no one took it. The server asked again, and no one said anything. The server then set the bill down on the table, and no one made any effort to pick it up. I was wondering, *Well who is paying for this?* I was invited as a guest, so I assumed I would not be paying the bill for this large group in this very expensive restaurant. But still no one said a word or moved to deal with the check. Finally, I got up and walked down to the end of the table, picked up the check, and said, "I will pay it." They all stared at me. "You are going to pay the whole check?" "Yes, I said." "Oh, thank you so much," they said." As the server came to get the card, one pastor said, "Hey, wait a minute. You are our guest. I will pay part of the bill."

As the meal broke up, suddenly, everyone began to speak to me. You know, many of those pastors never forgot that night. They were all invited to that dinner assuming that the meal would be paid for by the leaders of the event. And the leaders thought that it had been explained that every person there would pay for their own meal. So, everyone thought that someone else was paying, because most of them told me that if they had known they would be paying $100 to $130 per person for that dinner, they never would have gone. But I had some money and knew this was a great time to be generous on every occasion.

Drenda and I have funded ministry all over the world with our own money as well as having many partners stand beside us as we take the message of the Kingdom of God to the nations. It is not burdensome to do so as God is faithful to bring all the money we need when we need it. What I am trying to say is that having money is important.

Your vision needs to go beyond yourself. You already know that God loves you, and He wants you to have good things. But you're on assignment. You're His ambassador living in a specific location and on a specific mission. You are called to be effective in your assignment here in the land of poverty—like Joseph in Egypt, where by revelation he saved that nation. By revelation, you should be saving the people all around you too. By revelation, I mean you hear the plan, God leads you to the harvest, and there is money to get the job done. By revelation, you should be an island of light in the midst of darkness. People should be saying, "There's something about that person! I've got to have that! Let's go find out what it is!"

Drenda and I just had dinner as I was writing this chapter, and the server began telling us that she has some health issues and cannot afford health insurance. We know this woman as a woman of faith, but we never heard her mention this before. We do know that she had gone through a bit of depression during the winter months as she had told us on our previous visit. But then, I understood. Money problems and the lack of money bring on such stress and worry. I know. I was on antidepressants for fear when our money was nonexistent. We felt honored to give her a large tip that day and to be light to her of God's goodness.

Demonstrating the Kingdom

> *David left Gath and escaped to the cave of Adullam. When his brothers and his father's household heard about it, they went down to him there. All those who were in distress or in debt or discontented gathered around him, and he became their commander. About four hundred men were with him.*
> —1 Samuel 22:1–2

David had just defeated Goliath. And David was the only man in that kingdom who had the faith to face Goliath and tap into the covenant, the Kingdom of God, to defy and defeat that enemy. And now he was on the run because King Saul was so jealous of him that he was trying to kill him.

But David was soon joined by others. Some 400 men who were fearful, discouraged, in debt, and needing money followed after David. Why? Because he had the answer. They saw in David the answer they were looking for. They saw in him the direction that would take them out of the impoverished leadership they had through Saul. They saw a new direction for their lives and their country.

If you continue reading their story, you'll see that these men were mentored by David in the laws of faith. They began to prosper. In the end, we see in the book of Chronicles that these same men who were so discouraged and discontented were able to give $17 billion to the temple-building project. That is in today's money, of course. But think about what had happened to these men who were once in so much need that they followed David to a cave! They were transformed by the reality of an example!

You should have your own discipleship program like this going on. There should be people in your life who are discouraged, depressed, in debt, and have no direction. They're in survival mode, and they're looking for answers and a place where they can find truth—and they can find this in you, because where is the Kingdom of heaven? It's in you!

God is calling each of us to occupy a place, a planting of the Lord to display His splendor. God is going to call people to all kinds of places so His glory can be seen and draw people in. That splendor in you is going make you look different than the world looks and stand out with uniqueness and excellence. But we've got to get in gear. We have to get going, get into the right assignment, and then excel in it. But when you don't have the proper mindset of the Kingdom and your purpose, you'll just stop. You'll get your bills paid and then take a nap. But this is not you. I pray that the Holy Spirit births in you a vision for the Kingdom. I pray that you'll walk down the street and burst into tears from compassion for people's lives—and you'll pray, "God, give me a million dollars so I can give it away."

> **GOD IS CALLING EACH OF US TO OCCUPY A PLACE, A PLANTING OF THE LORD TO DISPLAY HIS SPLENDOR.**

Don't let people see how great your faith is only by what you have. Let them see how great your faith is by what you've given away.

Most people will earn money in order to get something for themselves, but let's become Kingdom-minded. It's not about us. We will stand before Jesus one day and give an account of what we did in this life—and it's not going to be the house we have or the faith we exercised to get a pair of shoes. It will be about the faith we use to get our assignments done for the Kingdom.

It's got to be all about the Kingdom.

And don't worry how you are going to pay for your assignment. God will show you how to fund it, how to harvest the money you need.

It takes faith for you to get up and go with God, to get the job done. And we have a lot of lazy Christians. We do. We grew up in America, and we sit at home waiting for God to do stuff for us.

We have this marvelous position in Christ as citizens of His great Kingdom and as members of God's household, but yet so many Christians are living like orphans, blaming others for where they're at in life while at the same time just expecting God to fix their situations. What they do not realize is that they are their problem. They see themselves as victims instead of victors. But not you, not now. Maybe that is how you used to be, but that was the old you. Now, you renewed your strength like the eagles, and you will do exploits in the name of Jesus. Yes, I am talking about you!

The Spirit of God in you has your answer. You just need a revelation of how great the potential in you is.

> *If God is for us, who can be against us? He who did not spare his own Son, but gave him up for us all—how will he not also, along with him, graciously give us all things? Who will bring any charge against those whom God has chosen? It is God who justifies. Who then is the one who condemns? No one. Christ Jesus who died—more than that, who was raised to life—is at the right hand of God and is also interceding for us. Who shall separate us from the love of Christ? Shall trouble or hardship or persecution or famine or nakedness or danger or sword? As it is written: "For your sake we face death all day long; we are considered as sheep to be slaughtered."*

> ___No, in all these things we are more than conquerors through___
> ___him who loved us.___ *For I am convinced that neither death nor*
> *life, neither angels nor demons, neither the present nor the fu-*
> *ture, nor any powers, neither height nor depth, nor anything*
> *else in all creation, will be able to separate us from the love of*
> *God that is in Christ Jesus our Lord.*
>
> —Romans 8:31b–39

Do you get it? You have been made more than a conqueror. Stop with the "Woe is me mindset," and start thinking and saying what God says about you.

Now don't be misled by Paul's detour to a quote from Psalm 44:22 which says:

> *Yet for your sake we face death all day long; we are considered*
> *as sheep to be slaughtered.*

Before you say, "That is how I feel, like a sheep with no future," before you call all your friends and have a pity party, I think you need to find out where that comment came from and why Paul was quoting it.

That quote comes out of Psalm 44, and I think you should read it so you can understand more of what Paul was saying here in Romans 8.

In the first part of Psalm 44, the writer was remembering all of the powerful things that God had done for the nation of Israel in the past. But then, he went into a rant against God, blaming Him for all of their problems and mad because God was not helping them like He did in the past.

> *But now you have rejected and humbled us; you no longer go out with our armies. You made us retreat before the enemy, and our adversaries have plundered us. You gave us up to be devoured like sheep and have scattered us among the nations. You sold your people for a pittance, gaining nothing from their sale. You have made us a reproach to our neighbors, the scorn and derision of those around us. You have made us a byword among the nations; the peoples shake their heads at us.*
>
> —Psalm 44:9–14

But it was not that God had abandoned them. It was they, the nation, that had abandoned God and turned back to idols. So, Paul quoted this Scripture:

> *"Yet for your sake we face death all day long; we are considered as sheep to be slaughtered."*

Then his next words were:

> **<u>"No, in all these things we are more than conquerors through him who loved us."</u>**

Notice the first word is a very loud, NO! None of these things shall overtake you. You have been made more than a conqueror.

If you do not know who you are, you will not step out into the big assignments that God has for you. Please understand that God is not going to abandon you or lead you into destruction.

I remember one night I was driving out to Coshocton, Ohio, in my diesel Peugeot. (I loved that car, but it's hard to explain why. It was bent and broken with over 200,000 miles on it, but believe me, we went through some battles together). I'd gone about 40 miles—I was already past Newark, which was about halfway there—when my fuel light came on.

It was nearly one o'clock in the morning, and you may remember back 30 years ago, you couldn't get diesel at every station. I didn't know the area well and had no idea where a station was that carried diesel. So, I had to decide if I wanted to keep going or turn around and go clear back to Columbus, where I knew I could get fuel. At that point, I knew I still had just enough fuel to get back to Columbus. And if I went farther, I could expect to run out of fuel before I reached my destination and be stranded. I began to pray in the Spirit. Everything in me wanted to head back to safety. But as I prayed, in my spirit, I heard, "Go on." Really? Did I hear that correctly? But I decided that it must indeed be the Holy Spirit, because everything in me was saying to turn back.

So, I went on. I went only about 50 yards and stopped. "This is crazy," I said out loud. "I know there's no fuel out this way. I've got to stop." So, I pulled over to the side of the road and sat there praying in the Spirit. I was about to turn around when I just happened to look to my right, out the window, and next to the car was a rusty sign attached to a rusty wire fence that said Joe's Diesel Fuel—Two Miles Ahead. The sign looked like it had been there for a number of years. I was shocked to see it, but at the same time, I did not know if it had been there from 20 years before or not.

I did recognize that it was incredible that I had just happened to stop my car right there next to the sign, which was only about six by nine inches in size. The sign was right at my window, Joe's Diesel Fuel. So again, I had to make a decision to go forward. If it was indeed there, would it be open this late? I decided to at least go the two miles and check it out. Up ahead, I saw another sign that said to turn right for Joe's Diesel. I got off onto the road the sign said to turn on and found this station/repair shop there. There was no way I would have ever seen it from the main road. It was a few hundred yards down this gravel road. I was encouraged as I saw that the lights were still on as I pulled in. Looking around, I saw a man in the shop, so I walked over to him and asked him if they were open. He said they were closing in two minutes. I filled my tank and went on to my destination, in awe of what had just happened.

I feel the Lord taught me a valuable lesson that day. "If you just hang with Me, just listen to My Spirit, and just let Me guide you, I'll show you what to do."

And I also realized that the Holy Spirit saved me from backtracking and turning back. How many times do we start out on something then, because of fear, we turn back? We're going to advance much faster by listening to His voice and avoiding the lost time and lost opportunities that backtracking will cost us.

I'm telling you that many times in life, you'll be faced with diffi-

THE KINGDOM OF HEAVEN IS IN YOU—AND SO YOU HAVE THE WISDOM OF GOD AND THE DIRECTION THAT YOU NEED IN EVERY SITUATION OF LIFE.

culties that may appear you don't have an answer for, but the Bible says that God has given you all things that pertain to life and godliness. And where do you find those answers? They are in you! The Kingdom of heaven is in you—and so you have the wisdom of God and the direction that you need in every situation of life.

"So, Gary, all this sounds great, but as you have been saying, it takes money to get things done. So, how do I find the money I need to walk out my assignment in life and demonstrate the Kingdom to those around me?"

Great question. There are many aspects to that answer, but all are found in the Kingdom of God. This book is going to talk about one method that God will use to fund your assignment. For most people, this is their answer. But there are many ways, and they are all dependent on your understanding of how the Kingdom of God works. That is why you must become a student of the Kingdom of God. Your success depends on it. Assuming you understand the basics of how money works in the Kingdom, then this book could be the very answer that will propel you into your answer. If you do not have a basic understanding of how the Kingdom works, then get my books and study them.

> **BUT FOR MOST PEOPLE, THE ANSWER TO THEIR MONEY PROBLEMS AND FUNDING ISSUES IS A KINGDOM BUSINESS!**

But for most people, the answer to their money problems and funding issues is a Kingdom business!

Simply put: **The answer is business!!!**

04

GETTING DOWN TO BUSINESS

I think most people have an idea what the word business means, but let's take a look at a rather formal explanation of what the word business means before we get started.

"The term business refers to an organization or enterprising entity engaged in commercial, industrial, or professional activities, organizing some sort of economic production of goods or services. It would include efforts and activities undertaken by individuals to produce and sell goods and services for profit."[5]

For this book, I am going to focus on that last part, where individuals produce and sell goods for a profit. By the way, I like that word profit, and so should you because that word is your answer.

5 Adam Hayes, "What is a business? Understanding different types and company sizes," https://www.investopedia.com/terms/b/business.asp, February 29, 2024

Let me ask you a question. Who controls the farmer's wealth? I think all of us know what farming is all about. We understand that a farmer plants and raises crops to sell for a profit. Now, let's go a little deeper into that statement. Who determines how much seed he plants? He does, of course. You see, a farmer chooses how much profit he wants by how many acres he plants. If he wants to make more money, he can plant more acreage. It is up to him.

NO ONE DETERMINES YOUR INCOME BUT YOU.

And this is how businesses run as well. No one determines your income but you.

Think about what I am saying. A business has the potential to produce as much money as you want. Now, that is a very simple explanation, but that is really the truth. But the majority of people do not understand that. And you would say, "Well, of course they do." And I would argue back, "No, they don't." The number one reason they don't is because they really do not understand how money is created. So, **where does money come from anyway?**

Well, to most people, it is the bank through a loan, their job, their parents, or the government. Okay, so let's assume you say, "I get my money from my job." Great, but where did your company get the money to pay you? And most people would more than likely say, "I don't know. How would I know that?" Right, that is the problem. Some people know where money comes from, and others don't.

It is like the sign I saw at my bank a couple of months ago. The sign was advertising their CD rates, and at the time, the rate on their CDs was about 1%. But right next to that sign was a sign that said, "If you need money, we are offering personal loans at 7.2%." I couldn't believe it. They were going to pay me only 1%, and my money would be the source of the funds they were lending out at 7.2%. That would be a 6.2% profit for them. Is that a big deal? You tell me. At 1%, $5,000 would grow to $6,739 over 30 years, but at 7.2% for that same 30-year period, it would grow to $40,254. If the bank loaned that money out on their Visa credit card at 23%, that same $5,000 would grow to $2,489,564. That's right, two and half million.

The issue is someone knows how money works, and the other does not. You can't win unless you know how money works and where it comes from. It's so sad that when most Christians need money, they just say, "God will provide." Yes, I agree He will, but how? Also, let's understand that God has no money. All the money in the earth realm is held or has been created by a country. This is evidenced by the currency you currently hold in your wallet or purse. If you look at it, it has a nation stamped on it, meaning it is under the jurisdiction of men. God has no authority or jurisdiction to take it from them and give it to you. So, knowing that, when you, being a Christian, get this big vision from God, and you look at the bill for that vision, you say, "God will provide." But friend, how is He going to do that? I am not trying to be disrespectful. God will absolutely provide, every time. But how and where is He going to do that?

Now, I understand at first you may not know. But eventually, you must know to throw your net out over there in the deep water or to go to the lake and catch a fish, and in its mouth you will find a coin; or to go and gather a lot of pots, and God will fill them with oil. Eventually, a plan will be revealed and details put in place so that you can capture the money you need. As I said in the introduction, we have a problem. No one seems to know where or how to find that money. Well, that is what you are going to learn in this book, how to create money.

But before we get into that, there are a few money basics that you first must understand. The first is this, that all—and, yes, I mean all—money is created in the marketplace, through buying and selling. Let me give you an example. Let's say that you want to create some money. So, you look for something to sell, right? But you do not have anything to sell, so you buy some wood for $200 and create four chairs that you sell for $200 each. By selling those four chairs, you now have $800 in your hands. You subtract your overhead, the price of the wood, which was $200, and you have made a profit of $600. But stop. That $600 did not exist in the marketplace before you made those chairs. There was only $200 worth of wood. You just created $600 that is now flowing through the marketplace. Of course, it can be much more complicated than that. That is just a simple example.

ALL MONEY IS CREATED IN THE MARKETPLACE.

I have a guy in my church who did exactly that. He needed some extra money, so he started buying wood and making lawn chairs on the side. That little business paid off all his credit cards in one year. He understood that his answer was business, and he could create as much money as he needed.

Now, we understand that something must be sold to create the wealth or paycheck you need. All money is created when something is sold. Well, you may say, "I am not in sales. I work as a security guard down at XYZ company and get paid by the hour, so I am not in sales." But you are in sales; yes, you are. Where did your company get the money to pay you? They got it by selling their services to a company that needed security services as they transported their daily receipts and deposits to the bank. Everyone is in sales in some way or another. This is great because that means you can create all the money you need if you know how the system works. Do you want to create wealth or just hope to find some? Or maybe you are planning that someone who has money will give some to you? Good questions. I hope you know the right answer.

THIS BOOK IS GOING TO HELP YOU REINVENT HOW YOU THINK AND HOW YOU LIVE!

This book is going to help you reinvent how you think and how you live! But first, I really need to mess with your head a bit more. Don't worry. This will not be too painful, I hope. But I need to deal with your stinking thinking one more time.

I drove into Columbus with my family a couple of years ago, and we were on the I-270 beltway at around 5:00 p.m. My kids were astonished. "Dad, what's happened?" they said. "Has there been a wreck? What's going on?"

"This is rush hour," I explained calmly. "Happens twice a day. These people you see out here have voluntarily signed up for this."

"You're kidding?"

"Don't worry," I told them. "You'll never do this. We're training you to be entrepreneurs. You'll be able to choose your own hours. These people like having other people tell them when they can come and go. They like having only two weeks off a year and having a stagnant income."

Well, to be truthful, they don't like it. But they have not been trained to think any differently. Today, everyone is taught to go to college and get a job. But I disagree with that advice. Yes, some may need to become trained for what they want to do, but most need to be trained, more importantly, to think like an entrepreneur. You see, back when this country was founded, no one had jobs. Everyone knew you had to have a business. They didn't come across the ocean to see if there were any good jobs here. In fact, there weren't any jobs here when they arrived. They had to create wealth. What would they do? Find the nearest teepee and ask for a job? There wasn't anything here. They had to create their own livelihood.

> **YOU'RE MADE IN THE IMAGE OF GOD. YOU'RE MEANT TO CHANGE AND AFFECT YOUR NATURAL CIRCUMSTANCES. YOU'RE MADE WITH THE ABILITY TO CREATE STUFF. TO CREATE YOUR FUTURE AND ALL THAT YOU NEED.**

That's how you were created to think. You're made in the image of God. You're meant to change and affect your natural circumstances. You're made with the ability to create stuff. To create your future and all that you need. And if you cry out to the Holy Spirit, He's going to bring you an answer and show you what to do. All of us were created to live with a mindset of unlimited potential. If we create it, we can enjoy it. That is what motivates people, and this is why America has been the most productive country that has ever existed. And you can create your own answer as well. Speaking of business, I want to take you to a Bible story where God told a woman who had no financial hope that business was her answer.

The wife of a man from the company of the prophets cried out to Elisha, "Your servant my husband is dead, and you know that he revered the Lord. But now his creditor is coming to take my two boys as his slaves."

Elisha replied to her, "How can I help you? Tell me, what do you have in your house?"

"Your servant has nothing there at all," she said, "except a small jar of olive oil."

Elisha said, "Go around and ask all your neighbors for empty jars. Don't ask for just a few. Then go inside and shut the door behind you and your sons. Pour oil into all the jars, and as each is filled, put it to one side."

She left him and shut the door behind her and her sons. They brought the jars to her and she kept pouring. When all the jars were full, she said to her son, "Bring me another one."

But he replied, "There is not a jar left." Then the oil stopped flowing.

She went and told the man of God, and he said, "Go, sell the oil and pay your debts. You and your sons can live on what is left."
—2 Kings 4:1–7

This is a great story! This woman went from being in debt and possibly losing her kids to being out of debt and wealthy in one day!!!! What was her answer? How did that happen? By being obedient to a crazy word from God and then from that, starting a business by the direction of that same word.

Her answer was business!

You do not understand? Yes, her answer was business. Give me a minute, and I will show you why I say that. First of all, after reading this story, you should have all kinds of bells and whistles going off in your head while you are scrambling to find a pen and paper to take notes. Because if she went from broke to blessed, so should you. How many times have you heard or read this story without realizing what it is telling you? Probably many, but not today. Today, you are reading this story with the understanding that the Kingdom is a kingdom that is governed by laws, and laws do not change and are not partial to any one person. What happened for her can happen for you.

AS A SPIRITUAL SCIENTIST, YOU ARE GOING TO LOOK FOR THE HIDDEN CLUES AS TO HOW THIS WOMAN TAPPED INTO THE KINGDOM'S INEXHAUSTIBLE RESOURCES.

Now, as a spiritual scientist, you are going to look for the hidden clues as to how this woman tapped into the Kingdom's inexhaustible resources. You serve the same God, and you have access to the same voice she heard, the voice of the Holy Spirit. "Oh no, Gary. It was Elisha who told her what to do." Well, who do you think told him what to tell her? Right! So, let's take a closer look at this story and see if we can identify what actually happened, what laws of the Kingdom were in play, so you can have a similar story in your life.

First, we identify her problem. She needs money, but how could she acquire some? She did what most people do. She went to someone who she thought had money and then told them her sad situation, hoping to find help. But her answer, and your clue, is hidden in the prophet's response.

> *Elisha replied to her, "How can I help you? Tell me, what do you have in your house?"*

> *"Your servant has nothing there at all," she said, "except a small jar of olive oil."*

Amazingly, and probably in a bit of shock as to the question, she answered that she had nothing at all except a small jar of olive oil. I am sure her answer was meant to reinforce the fact that she, indeed, had no way of paying her debt off and again hoped for some help from Elisha. Then, what did the prophet tell her?

> *Elisha said, "Go around and ask all your neighbors for empty jars. Don't ask for just a few."*

Elisha did not agree with her assessment of the situation. He saw her answer in her situation.

Oh, if only we could learn to see what Elisha saw!

He saw a plan, a Holy Spirit plan that would provide all that she would need. He was not looking at that little bit of oil through the eyes of man's limitation. He was looking at that oil through the lens of the laws of the Kingdom. Do not think this is strange.

> **BUT WE MUST TAKE THE TIME TO LEARN KINGDOM LAW OR WE WILL BE LIMITED TO ACCEPT WHATEVER WE SEE WITH OUR EYES.**

A farmer who needs money does not look at his wagonful of seeds and say, "I am bankrupt. This seed will never pay my current bills." No, he looks at that seed through his understanding of the laws of nature, knowing that he can plant that seed and have wagons and wagons full of seed that would easily pay off his bills. The reason people do not do that is because they have only had their minds trained in the natural law. But we must take the time to learn Kingdom law or we will be limited to accept whatever we see with our eyes. Next, Elisha gave her the plan.

> *"Then go inside and shut the door behind you and your sons. Pour oil into all the jars, and as each is filled, put it to one side."*

Now, you would have to admit, that is a crazy plan! He was telling her that the very thing that she had admitted was not enough, in fact, was at a critical level, was the same thing that would become her deliverance. Wow! But you also would have to admit that it would take great faith to follow those instructions. Let's put this in perspective. She had never seen oil just appear before. She was going to have to explain to all her neighbors why she wanted to borrow their pots. They probably also knew how broke she was. And she knew they were also going to say she was crazy! But in faith, she went and borrowed the pots, put her pride aside, and just as the prophet had said, the oil multiplied.

Now, here is the next thing you must understand. The oil was not her answer. I know, you are going to say, "Yes, it was her answer." And I can agree, but not completely. And if you do not understand why I am saying this, then you may miss your answer also. Remember, she needed money to pay off a debt, so here comes the next instruction.

Elisha said, "*Go, sell the oil and pay your debts. You and your sons can live on what is left*" (2 Kings 4:7).

The oil was not her answer. Remember, she needed money. Selling off the oil for money was her answer. She had to monetize the harvest of her obedience. So, let me paraphrase what he was saying to her.

Go into the oil business! Sell the oil.

From what you sell, pay your debts.

I love that sentence. This is what business offers you too. We need to understand that even though she had pots full of oil, they still were not meeting her needs. She then had to sell the oil to have the money that she needed.

She had to do what? Sell the oil!

This is business.

This was the answer God gave her—business. Soon, she became known as the oil lady in her town. When anyone needed oil, they thought of her. They would go down to her house, and they bought oil. God gave her a business. She controlled it, she owned it, and she wasn't at the mercy of anyone else. It was her business, and she dictated how it operated. She was free to charge whatever she wanted for that oil. It was her business.

Now, you may say, "Well, I don't have any experience." She didn't either. She had probably never been in the oil business before. That's something to figure out once you've got pots full of oil. You can figure it all out when the grace starts to flow. You can get some knowledge and wisdom and hire accountants to handle the tax stuff. Don't let any of that scare you—just start thinking about where you're going to put all that oil.

How would you like to go to church so blessed that your family had to drive over in three cars just to have room for all the cash you were bringing for the offering? You'd open your Bible, and ten or twenty hundred-dollar bills would fall out. What if you were so prosperous you didn't have room for all the money that just kept pouring in?

Do you know why we don't see many Christians with this problem? The same reason we didn't see her with this problem. Because most of the church today is hanging on for a ride. They are acting like the tail when God says they are the head. They're still in survival mode, just getting the leftovers. If you don't like the sights and sounds of where you're hanging right now, you need to hang somewhere else. You just need to hang around some different folks. You need to hang around people that have vision. You need to start talking about vision. You need to start talking and praying in the Spirit and asking God to give you a revelation of something you can do. And you've got to stay there and pray long enough until you hear from Him. And when God shows you where you can operate in a mode of unlimited potential, then you've got to walk it out.

> **IF YOU DON'T LIKE THE SIGHTS AND SOUNDS OF WHERE YOU'RE HANGING RIGHT NOW, YOU NEED TO HANG SOMEWHERE ELSE.**

We need to stop here and talk a bit about that phrase, unlimited potential. We all were created with that concept built inside us. But this woman in the story missed that word as so many people do. You see, that woman was given a blank check, so to speak. "Go gather pots and not a few." Through the prophet, God was telling her to think big. There is a gusher of oil coming, and you get to decide how much you want. We can tell from the story that she was thrilled to see the oil fill all of her pots, because after exhausting her supply of pots, she asked for another one. But her son said there were no more, then the oil stopped. Do you want to know what she felt like

> **AND WHEN GOD SHOWS YOU WHERE YOU CAN OPERATE IN A MODE OF UNLIMITED POTENTIAL, THEN YOU'VE GOT TO WALK IT OUT.**

at that moment? Sick to her stomach. She then had the revelation that, yes, God was going to fill as many pots as she could find. Yes, the story ends well. She paid off her debt and saved her family.

You really could not have a better ending than that, right? Wrong! If only she would have realized that she held the key to the oil flow. She could have taken the time to amass hundreds, maybe even thousands, of pots, and not only could she have sold enough oil to pay her debt off, but she also could have bought houses and land for her boys to be held until they were married. Or she could have bought houses to rent out, or she could have paid off all her town's debt. The possibilities are endless. But do you want to know why she did not think that way? Because all she was thinking about was the debt and her sons. She was focused on getting enough oil to pay that off and free her sons, and she missed the opportunity of a lifetime.

Let me translate that for you, her survival thinking was the problem. The answer for her life was staring her in the face, and she could not see it. I am sure that the answer for your life is staring you in the face as well. Can you see it? "But Gary, I do not have a prophet standing here and telling me what I should do." You are correct. You have someone greater, the Holy Spirit and the Word of God.

The woman with the oil still had to sell that oil. And you'll have to do your thing too. You'll have to change. You'll have to start thinking differently. You'll have to figure out what you're doing and throw out your net. I bet you'll be upset once the grace starts flowing and you find out that sister so-and-so was wise enough to plant 3,000 acres, and you've only prepared a little three-foot by three-foot plot!

You have to get out there and take that thing by force. You just need to jump in and hang on.

So, the next time you are at church and the pastor says it is time to receive the offering, look at what you are giving and ask yourself this, "Do I want to protect the seed or the harvest? Am I going to see what Elisha saw? Am I going to look past the natural and see the hand of God?"

> **YOU HAVE TO GET OUT THERE AND TAKE THAT THING BY FORCE. YOU JUST NEED TO JUMP IN AND HANG ON.**

To have a Kingdom business, you must start thinking that way.

Let me tell you a story of a woman who did just that and changed not only her own life but also a town's life.

Cordia Harrington was a young, divorced mother with three children looking for a way to make income. She was a real estate agent with $587 to her name. As a real estate agent, she was disappointed with the quality of the homes she was selling and decided that she could do a better job. She started her own home construction business and also was then able to sell them. But the construction business was taking her away from her kids too often, so she began to look for something that would give her more time. She felt that owning a McDonald's franchise would be the answer. She sold her construction business and opened a McDonald's in a town that had 10,000 people in it. To increase her business, she bought a Greyhound bus franchise and put it across the street. One hundred and twenty buses a day came to the bus depot, which boosted her McDonald's sales to one of the top McDonald's in the nation. So, she bought two more McDonald's.

Her aha moment struck, strangely enough, after she was nominated in 1992 to be on the McDonald's bun committee. The experience opened her eyes to business possibilities. As she traveled the world looking at bakeries, she would carry a notepad and make many notes on how to run a bakery. When McDonald's decided it wanted a new bun supplier, Harrington became determined to win the contract, even though she had no experience running a bakery or owning a bakery. "You see a tiny crack in the door, and you have to run through it," she says. "I really believed I could do this."

Harrington studied the bakery business and made sure she was never off the executives' radar. "If you have a dream, you can't wait for people to call you," she says. "So, I'd visit a mill and send them photos of myself in a baker's hat and jacket holding a sign that said, 'I want to be your baker.'" After 4 years and 32 interviews, her persistence paid off.

Harrington sealed the deal with a handshake, sold her franchises, invested everything she owned, and borrowed $13.5 million. She was ready to build the fastest, most automated bakery in the world. The Tennessee Bun Company opened ahead of schedule in 1997, in time for a slump in U.S. fast-food sales for McDonald's. Before Harrington knew it, she was down to her last $20,000, not enough to cover payroll. And her agreement with McDonald's required that she sell exclusively to the company. "I cried myself to sleep many nights," she recalls. "I really did think, *I am going to go bankrupt.*

But Harrington worked out an agreement to supply Pepperidge Farm as well. "McDonald's could see a benefit if our production went up and prices went down, and no benefit if we went out of business," she says. "That deal saved us."

Over the next eight years, Harrington branched out even more: She started her own trucking business, added a cold-storage company, and now has three bakeries producing fresh buns and frozen dough—all now known as the Bun Companies.

Speed is still a priority: It takes 11 people at the main bakery to turn out 60,000 buns an hour for clients across 40 states, South America, and the Caribbean.

"This is more than a job," says Harrington. "It's a mission. I'm always thinking, *How can we best serve our employees?* If we support them, they'll do their best to look after our clients. That's how it works here."[6]

Most people come into a fast-food environment with the thought that they are there to get somewhere else. They do not stop to consider that they are working in one of the biggest companies in the nation. If they did, they would be taking notes, just like Cordia did. How processes and ordering are done and how payroll

6 "Cordia Harrington: From Rags to Riches Success Story," moneyminting.blogspot.com, May 25, 2011

and onboarding are done. So many things to be learned right in front of them. I always say that God does not waste experience and there are no small assignments.

BE OPEN AND WATCH FOR THE HOLY SPIRIT TO SPEAK TO YOU WHEN YOU LEAST EXPECT IT.

When you are thinking right, you catch those moments where ideas pop into your head. But slaves do not look for those thoughts. They reject them as they imply more labor or expense would be required. But not you. Be open and watch for the Holy Spirit to speak to you when you least expect it.

Your answer may be right in front of your face!

CHAPTER FIVE

SOLUTIONS PAY BIG MONEY

Here is a statement that is surely true: people get paid to fix a problem. The bigger the problem you fix, the more you will make. Most people try to avoid problems, but not you. You are going to look for them. As I said earlier, every business is in business because it fixes someone's problem. Some of the biggest companies are companies that have fixed a huge problem. For instance, let's take a look at Amazon. Sure, people complain about them, but as much as we want to complain about how big they are and how they are hurting the small retail stores, what they do is absolutely incredible. Think about it. In the past, if I needed a computer cartridge for my printer, I would have had to drive to a retail store to buy one. That is time and money on my part. But now, I click a button, and within a day, and sometimes the same day, the cartridge shows up at my house with no shipping fees. It is no wonder they captured 37.5% of the online retail market in 2023.[7] You would have to agree, they have solved a huge problem. But the problem you want to fix does not need to be on such a grand scale to be effective.

My family has owned pizza shops in my hometown for the last 50 years. I helped my dad start the business when I was a sophomore in high school and ran one of his two shops for a few years before I went to college. His pizza shops have been a huge success and changed the financial climate of our family in a huge way. My dad worked in a warehouse for years, which he hated. He had no experience in the pizza business, but one day, he found out that the little pizza shop that we ordered from on a weekly basis was going up for sale. My dad was hesitant to really consider it, but my mom thought it would be a great idea. With some persuasion, my dad went into the pizza business. It was a big success.

He then bought an old grocery store and converted it to a bigger and better pizza shop with indoor dining and a lunch menu. Previously, his shop was only open in the evenings and was pickup only. Then, he opened a second shop a couple of years later in a nearby town. The two pizza shops made my dad wealthy, which again had a huge impact on our family. And it was a great experience working in the family business. I loved it. I saw right away that business changed my family's life, and I always considered it the way to go.

So, let's answer a question: why were my dad's pizza shops successful? In simple terms, he was solving a problem. People

---

7 Geri Meleva, "Amazing Amazon Statistics You Need to Know to Amplify Growth in 2023," Influencermarketinghub.com, October 24, 2023

are hungry, and they need to eat. My dad offered great food at a reasonable price, so the people came back for more. He told me that he would always stay in business because people get hungry every day, and he would solve that problem every day. He felt he could not fail, and he didn't.

Now, of course, there are many issues that will determine if a business succeeds or fails besides just opening your doors. But for our simple explanation, businesses solve someone's problem. McDonald's is in business because people are hungry. Your plumber is in business to fix someone's problem, perhaps a broken pipe. The accountant is in business because people do not know how to do their taxes. So, let's stop and think about this for a minute and see if you can identify an area where you think you could help or bring a solution.

1. Name something you see that is a problem most people have.
2. What injustice do you want to correct?
3. What need do you want to meet?
4. What is your passion?
5. What can you do?

I had a guy come up to me at church after I had been teaching along these lines. He wanted me to pray with him that God would show him a business idea. He had some experience in drywall work and began to formulate a business based on a problem he saw in the drywall industry. Most of the guys he knew in the business sure knew how to hang drywall, but he recognized that there were a ton of people out there who didn't need drywall hung. No, what they needed was to have some drywall patched. Life can be hard on drywall. If you move a hanging light, it leaves a hole in the ceiling. If you need to fix a frozen pipe, it leaves a hole in the drywall. Over the years in most homes, things happen, and you will have a few holes in your drywall.

For instance, my son was wrestling with a friend and accidentally punched a good-sized hole in the wall. I am really not good with drywall. I never seem to be able to get the mud smooth enough so the seams won't be noticeable. Plus, I hate the dust, and having to cut and measure it is just a hassle. So, in our case, concerning the big hole in our wall, we just put a picture over it.

Anyway, this guy in my church put together a business plan to attack this narrow drywall market. And you know what? He is doing great and is now expanding his business into other states. He saw a problem and found a way to monetize it.

BUSINESS WAS MY ANSWER OUT OF OVERWHELMING DEBT AND HOPELESSNESS!

Business was my answer out of overwhelming debt and hopelessness!

When I came out of college, I had no idea what I was going to do. I knew that I had a call into the ministry, but I had no idea where that would lead. When God led me to go to Oral Roberts University, I was faithful to go, but He never told me what would come after that. But without going into a long story, strangely, just out of college, as I mentioned, God led me to go into financial sales for a fairly young financial company at the time. I had no experience in sales, and did not even like the idea of being in sales, but I was sure that God was leading me to take that step.

If you know my background before college, I was shy and never comfortable around people. This position would require me to get my own leads, and I would be paid completely from the commissions I generated. There was no salary. And most importantly, I would be talking to people. It made no sense to me at the time, but I understand why God led me down that path now. I had to overcome my fear of people if I would ever be able to fulfill God's call on my life. Somehow, even though I was afraid to step into that position, something on the inside of me was fascinated by the financial field. So, I said yes, got my life insurance license, and launched out.

At that time, I was installing draperies and mini blinds for a company, and since I had no one to call or talk to that I knew in Tulsa, I asked my boss if he would mind if I called some of the people that I had met while working for him. And he said that would be fine. So, that is what I did. I can remember the first night that I stayed in the office late so that I could make some calls. That was tough, but I did make a few, and I set one appointment who ended up buying from me. I got better at this as time went on, and, eventually, I was promoted to Regional Vice President and then to Senior Vice President. But I was still just barely making a living and falling farther and farther into debt.

But then I can remember the day that God said, "Now is the time to step out on your own and launch your own financial company, one that would honor Me and help people." The company that I worked for did not allow us to talk to people about the Lord. But God was leading me to start my own company? I balked a little. I really did not want to continue to sell insurance and securities. I had been doing that full-time for the last 11 years, and I wanted to do something more meaningful. But yet, I felt that God was telling me to stay in the financial field.

At that time, Drenda and I were in debt and struggling, and we were just starting to learn about the Kingdom of God and how it worked. But we only had a glimpse of it at that time. God was leading us, and we knew that learning about the Kingdom was our answer. And although we saw many things happening as we pursued God's directive to learn about the Kingdom and how it works, we still were missing so many pieces of the puzzle. But something happened that changed my attitude toward where God was leading me.

When we first came to Ohio, I continued working with the company that I had been working with in Tulsa while I put together some ideas for my own company. I really wanted to help my clients with a fuller picture of financial health than just selling them securities and insurance. I wanted to include what I was learning about the Kingdom as well. And I wanted to somehow help families with their debt. So, I put together some concepts and launched my new company, and we named it Innovative Financial Concepts. In a sense, I was doing what I had been doing in Tulsa but added a few areas of business to that model. But as I got about a month into this new company, I knew something was wrong. It just did not feel right. I knew that there was more that God wanted me to do with this company.

About this time, God gave me a dream in the night concerning what I was to do. In this dream, I saw a caterpillar climbing up a branch, and out on the end of it, the caterpillar spun a cocoon. Then, out of the cocoon came this beautiful butterfly. Next in the dream, I heard the Lord say, "The business I am calling you to build will not look like the other one. As the caterpillar is to the butterfly, so shall your business be." I do not remember the exact verbiage He used now, but that was pretty close. I understood what He was saying, but I had no idea that what was going to happen would drastically change my business from crawling, the caterpillar, to flying, the butterfly.

At this time, I was making cold calls every morning to find my clients. I would make 90 cold calls a day out of the telephone book. (Do you remember those days?) Out of those 90 calls, I would usually set about two to three appointments.

One of those appointments was with a man named Dave. I remember going to his home and sitting down with him and his wife. As I started to get into my presentation about insurance and investments, they admitted that they were broke. They were just hanging on financially. The wife burst into tears, and I realized that the issue was not going to be insurance and investments. They had no money for either.

So, I began to tell them a little about the Kingdom of God and some of what Drenda and I were learning. I told them about my deer hunting and that God had taught me how to receive instead of hunting in my own strength. I also shared what I was learning about faith and the Kingdom. More importantly, I also shared with them what God told me, that I was in this financial mess because we had never learned how His Kingdom operated. I knew the Kingdom was their answer also.

Whenever I meet new clients, I always have them fill out a data sheet, which is just a brief profile of where they are at financially. That way, I would know how much insurance they might need and if there were any investments that might need to be looked at. When I reviewed their data sheet, I could see it was not good. I felt so bad for them as I hated debt and was just learning how to come out of it myself.

I set a second appointment with them and told them I would go back to the office and see what I could find that might help. Actually, I did not have anything back in my office that could help. All I had to offer was insurance and securities, which were not an option for them. But I felt such compassion for them that I decided that there must be something I could do to help them. My decision to look deeper was not motivated by my expectation of somehow finding some money that could produce a sale. I knew that any money I might find was needed to go toward their negative monthly budget. Leaving their house, I had no idea if there was any money that I could free up or not, and I really did not have any idea of where to look. But on the way home as I was praying about this, I really felt impressed to look at what they were spending and find out if there were cheaper options out there that might free up some monthly cash flow.

So, that week I spent my time making calls, looking through the yellow pages (equivalent to today's Google search, except it was a book and not online). I checked on every monthly expense they had and compared it to other companies' rates and products. Slowly, I found some options for them to look at that would save them some money. But I was shocked that when I had completed my survey and added it all up, I had found over $500 a month in freed up cash. I then took my financial calculator and added that $500 to their debt payments, thus accelerating their payoffs. When I hit the compute button, I sat there in shock. My calculator indicated that they could be out of debt in 6.2 years. I remember thinking that I must have made a mistake and went through the whole calculation again with the same answer.

Then, I went to my file drawer and pulled out a couple of my other clients' files as I had a data sheet on all my clients. I began the same process, and without exception, all of them could be out of debt in 5 to 7 years, including their home mortgage, without changing their income. I remember then thinking, *If this is true, why isn't anyone telling people this?*

I was so excited to tell Dave and his wife what I found. So, I typed up a sheet with all their numbers on it and also the total time needed to be totally debt free at the bottom. When I went back to see them, I told them that I thought they would be pleased with what I had discovered. I pulled the sheet out and started going down the list of where I thought they could free up money. I kept the entire list covered, only revealing each item as I came to it. Throughout this reveal, they were getting happier and happier. When I ended, showing them that they could be completely debt free, including their home mortgage, in 6.2 years without changing their income, they started crying, jumped up from the table, ran around, and gave me a hug. They were so happy.

That visit changed me, and I knew that this was what the new company was supposed to do. This was the new company that God was showing me, showing people how to be free from debt and learning how to prosper in His Kingdom. We changed the name of the company from Innovative Financial Concepts to Faith-Full Family Finances, then to Forward Financial Group about 10 years ago. That company has now been in existence for over 30 years. Counting the company I worked for in Tulsa, I have been involved with financial services for 43 years now and still love it.

You may wonder whatever happened to Dave. Well, he was so impressed with what we did for him that he worked in our company for about a year or so on a part-time basis. I kept up with him for a number of years but have lost track of him recently.

By the way, as I mentioned in chapter three, we still do a Get Out of Debt Plan free of charge for anyone who asks. We also specialize in helping our clients safeguard their investments from losing principal. I am proud to say that we have invested hundreds of millions of dollars for our clients, and not one person has lost a single penny due to market fluctuations. We went on to hire and train associates and began operating in every state except New York. Today, the company still produces hundreds of thousands of dollars a year in profit. So yes, having a business radically changed our family and delivered us out of debt—thank you, Jesus!

People ask me, "Was it hard? Did you ever have days you wanted to quit?" Absolutely, I had days I wanted to quit. But I always remembered what my pastor said in Tulsa. If you hear the voice of God give you direction, do not move from that directive until

He speaks again. Oh, there were times in those early days when I was listening pretty hard, waiting for permission to change assignments. But, of course, He did not change His mind. Yes, it was hard; there was a lot to learn. But business was our answer.

What about my call to preach?

Well, when I was 40 years old, God spoke to me at a Sunday night service and said, "Now is the time I want you to launch a church here in New Albany, Ohio, and teach them what I have taught you about the Kingdom." I asked the Lord, "Should I close my business?" He said, "No, it helps many." So, for these past 29 years, I have pastored my church, Faith Life Church, and also maintained and run my company. I do not see it as a conflict as all of it is ministry in my mind. The ministry itself has expanded into over 70 nations, is on daily TV in every time zone in the world, and people are being set free and learning about the Kingdom of God. It is awesome. The company also keeps growing as more and more people find themselves in debt, and investors are afraid to put their money in the market or even the banks. By the way, if you want to reach my company, you can do so by calling 1-(888)-397-3328 or going to ForwardFinancialGroup.com.

06

ANYONE CAN CATCH FISH IF JESUS TELLS THEM WHERE AND HOW!

In Luke Chapter 5, we find an amazing story that you need to read with a Kingdom mindset, because within it are valuable lessons that you will need to understand. I know the story is a bit long, but please take the time to read it.

> *One day as Jesus was standing by the Lake of Gennesaret, the people were crowding around him and listening to the word of God. He saw at the water's edge two boats, left there by the*

fishermen, who were washing their nets. He got into one of the boats, the one belonging to Simon, and asked him to put out a little from shore. Then he sat down and taught the people from the boat.

When he had finished speaking, he said to Simon, "Put out into deep water, and let down the nets for a catch."

Simon answered, "Master, we've worked hard all night and haven't caught anything. But because you say so, I will let down the nets."

When they had done so, they caught such a large number of fish that their nets began to break. So they signaled their partners in the other boat to come and help them, and they came and filled both boats so full that they began to sink.

When Simon Peter saw this, he fell at Jesus' knees and said, "Go away from me, Lord; I am a sinful man!" For he and all his companions were astonished at the catch of fish they had taken, and so were James and John, the sons of Zebedee, Simon's partners.

Then Jesus said to Simon, "Don't be afraid; from now on you will fish for people." So they pulled their boats up on shore, left everything and followed him.

—Luke 5:1–11

Okay, there is much revelation in this story. It is a story about business, and within it are secrets of the Kingdom that will set your business apart. So, let me take some time and help you understand the laws of the Kingdom that are evident in this story.

First, we know that Simon Peter, James, and John were professional fisherman. They had been fishing all their lives. They also had been raised on the Sea of Galilee and knew it like the back of their hands. But this night, they went out and caught nothing. I suppose you could say, "Well, that happens. You can't have a great night of fishing every night." Maybe, but then a Rabbi, not a fisherman, walked by and asked to borrow their boat so that He could push off of shore a little and teach the people who were there. Okay, that part makes sense. After all, they were already done fishing for the day and were washing their nets. But it is what happened after Jesus taught that should catch your attention. Jesus told Peter to:

"Put out into deep water, and let down the nets for a catch."

What? A Rabbi was telling Peter how to fish? Peter was taken aback by it.

Simon answered, "Master, we've worked hard all night and haven't caught anything. But because you say so, I will let down the nets."

At first, Peter was telling Jesus that they had already been fishing all night and had not caught anything. But Jesus was not only telling Peter to throw out his nets, but also, He was telling him exactly where to throw them.

Please make a note here. You must remember this.

Jesus told Peter where the fish were!

The result?

> When they had done so, they caught such a large number of fish that their **nets began to break**. So they signaled their partners in the other boat to come and help them, and they came and **filled both boats so full that they began to sink**.

That is one heck of a catch. In fact, the Bible says they were all shocked.

> When Simon Peter saw this, he fell at Jesus' knees and said, "Go away from me, Lord; I am a sinful man!" For he and all his companions **were astonished at the catch of fish they had taken, and so were James and John, the sons of Zebedee, Simon's partners**.

They were all astonished! Even though they had fished all their lives, they had never seen anything like that before.

You can imagine the commotion that caused at the fish market. Everyone would be wanting to know how that happened. Exactly! And that is the question you had better be asking right now: "How did that happen?" Oh, I know what you will say. "Jesus did it." But you must remember that Jesus laid aside His former glory and came to earth as a man.

> Christ himself was like God in everything. But he did not think that being equal with God was something to be used for his

own benefit. But he gave up his place with God and made him-
self nothing. He was born as a man and became like a servant.
And when he was living as a man, he humbled himself and was
fully obedient to God, even when that caused his death—death
on a cross.

—Philippians 2:6–8 (NCV)

In fact, the Bible calls Him the Son of Man during His ministry, and when the demons called Him the Son of God, He rebuked them and told them to be quiet. Thus, He had to be baptized with the Holy Spirit at the River Jordan to have the ability to do the works of God, just as you do. No, we cannot say it was Jesus, who He was, that brought the fish. Rather, Jesus was demonstrating Kingdom law, and we need to look at the story to discern the Kingdom laws that were in operation. I am sure you would like to have the kind of success they had that day; and you can, over and over again.

So, let's ask this question, "How did they catch those fish?" That question is really no different than me asking you how an airplane flies or why your room lights up when you flip a switch. Why? Because you know that physical laws explain how a jet flies. You also know that anyone who understands those laws can duplicate them wherever and whenever they want to and fly. However, most people would say it was a miracle. But I disagree. Look at the definition of the word miracle from the *Oxford English Dictionary*.

Miracle: a highly <u>improbable</u> or <u>extraordinary</u> event, development, or accomplishment that brings very welcome consequences.

I submit to you that this event was not improbable or extraordinary from heaven's perspective. I believe the supernatural is natural in the Kingdom of God. But because we have been trained our entire lives in how the earth, the physical realm, operates, we are shocked at this event and call it a miracle. However, until you see it as normal, until you gain confidence in the laws of God's Kingdom, you will always doubt what you have not seen and will have a hard time receiving from God. But the more you study these laws of the Kingdom, the more comfortable and confident you will get in trusting them to work every time. We can fly a man to the moon because we are confident in the physical laws of nature. The laws of the Kingdom are just as unchanging and sure. Once we learn them, we can then use them whenever we need to.

I BELIEVE THE SUPERNATURAL IS NATURAL IN THE KINGDOM OF GOD.

BUT THE MORE YOU STUDY THESE LAWS OF THE KINGDOM, THE MORE COMFORTABLE AND CONFIDENT YOU WILL GET IN TRUSTING THEM TO WORK EVERY TIME.

So, as I said earlier, pay very close attention to stories like this one. Until you can explain how and why those fish showed up, you cannot duplicate that situation. You will never be able to live what you cannot teach. And do not be in such awe over this story. You will have many stories just like this. So, let's go back to our question.

How did those fish show up?

On the surface of this question, we see that Jesus Himself told them where and how to fish, over there in the deep water, and to use their nets. He gave them a very specific plan of action in regard to location and method. He also clearly identified what they were after, fish. I know all of this may seem trivial and obvious, but these things are huge. As I said in the title of this chapter, anyone can catch fish if Jesus tells them where the fish are and the method to be used to catch them.

> **JESUS TOLD THEM WHERE THE FISH WERE—HE WILL ALSO TELL YOU!**

Jesus told them where the fish were—He will also tell you!

But there is a lot in this story that you need to know. So, we will look at it slowly and thoroughly. First, we can see that Jesus told them where, location, and secondly, how, the nets. I believe the nets are the first thing we should look at because the nets will play a huge role in knowing the location. As you know, there are many ways to catch fish: bait on a single hook, bait on a big treble hook, lures, traps, nets, and the list goes on and on.

Jesus gave Peter a very clear message regarding the method to use when harvesting his fish: use your nets. Now, this brings up a couple of things that you must know regarding nets, the method of harvest. Before you go fishing, you need to know if your harvest requires a net, a single hook, or a real estate license and pen and paper. Your method of harvesting will be determined by what you are wanting to harvest.

What exactly does your harvest look like?

Let's look past the fish for a moment. In reality, Peter and his team were not really fishing for fish but for money. Meaning that they knew they would sell the fish they caught for the money they needed. Now, pay attention to what I am saying. Many people ask God for money. But unless they can define what their harvest looks like, nothing will happen. God has no money. When we ask God for the money we need, He will most likely do the same thing He did for Peter and the team. He will tell us to go and catch a fish, go and start a business, or go and sell something. He is going to give you direction in regard to capturing or creating the money you need.

> **BUT UNLESS THEY CAN DEFINE WHAT THEIR HARVEST LOOKS LIKE, NOTHING WILL HAPPEN.**

If you do not know what your harvest looks like, how will you know how to catch it?

Okay, I see you are confused, so let me back up. Let's say you are not a fisherman but a real estate agent. Your nets would be the listings you obtain or the houses you sell. Your nets would look different than Peter's fishing nets, but they would be nets all the same. Your nets would be homes you have listed for sale on the Internet, in the paper, or in magazines. They would be your office receiving phone calls from signs that they have seen at a home you have listed. Those are your nets. But again, if you did not have a defined harvest, in your case, selling a house, how would you know what kind of nets to put out?

Many times, I will be talking to people who are telling me how they want to prosper and this and that, and I will stop them and ask them where their nets are. They usually just stare at me a minute. I tell them that I own a house up in Nova Scotia in a fishing village where they catch lobsters and crabs. I tell them that those lobster fishermen mark every spot they drop a lobster trap on their GPS. They know exactly where to check for their harvest.

Then I ask again, "Where are your nets? What can God fill? How can He get the money to you?" And guess what? Unfortunately, most of the time when I talk to people, they cannot define what their harvest looks like, let alone where they have placed nets. So obviously, sadly, they have no harvest. Then, they get disappointed with God and think He has failed them.

Of course, just having a job is a net, but it is usually a stagnant one, unable to respond to sudden demands for money or the funding of an unexpected, sudden assignment. That is why I like to tell people that it is possible to have many different nets all catching harvests at the same time, which is a model I like.

Okay, let's go a little deeper with this. Let's assume you have no idea what your harvest looks like. You know you need money but have no idea what kind of harvest would produce what you need. What would you do?

That is a great question and one I get a lot. To answer that question, I would like to bounce off of another fishing story in the Bible, but hold on to Luke chapter 5. We are not even close to ending our discussion on that chapter.

But so that we may not cause offense, go to the lake and throw out your line. Take the first fish you catch; open its mouth and you will find a four-drachma coin. Take it and give it to them for my tax and yours.

—Matthew 17:27

Peter had taxes to pay but had no money to pay them. I think we can all relate to that at least one time in our lives. This time, Jesus actually told him to **go catch a fish**.

Jesus was actually telling him what his harvest looked like.

Again, Peter did not need fish; he needed money. "Go and catch a fish!" "No, Jesus, you do not understand. I need my tax money." "Peter, go and catch a fish!" If your occupation was plumbing, it might sound something like this. "Go to XYZ builder, and tell him you would like to plumb a house for him." If you were in sales, it might sound like this, "Go and talk to this person," or "Call back that client that said no the last time." You get the idea. The harvest is not money, but instead, it is usually something that will be converted to money. This is the key.

THE HARVEST IS NOT MONEY, BUT INSTEAD, IT IS USUALLY SOMETHING THAT WILL BE CONVERTED TO MONEY.

Stop waiting for someone to hand you money, and stop telling your sad story of having no money to all your friends. That is unbelief and fear. Listen, Jesus will tell you where the fish are at, where your harvest is at, just like He did for Peter.

Drenda and I were in that state for years. No money, and we had no idea how to get any. But when we began to study the Kingdom, we realized that we were not without answers. The Holy Spirit told Jesus where the fish were at, and He could do it again. So, we sowed a seed and asked the Lord for help in showing us how to get out of the mess we were in.

STOP WAITING FOR SOMEONE TO HAND YOU MONEY, AND STOP TELLING YOUR SAD STORY OF HAVING NO MONEY TO ALL YOUR FRIENDS.

When God spoke to me about starting my business, helping people get out of debt and safeguarding their investments, I knew the market was huge. Everyone was in debt. I also knew that God was showing me my harvest, NOT THE MONEY but how I was going to capture money from the marketplace. Although God gave me the plan, showing people how to get out of debt, in the beginning, I was not sure how to monetize what I was doing. But I knew I was onto something big. I knew I could not, or I should say I did not, want to charge people for showing them what I knew about getting out of debt. I wanted to make the plan free. As I continued to pray about it, God began to show me how to monetize the plan yet offer it for free to the consumer. Once I had that laid out, I knew it was over. Even though I had not made any money yet in the new company, I knew that my money problems were over. In fact, in two and a half years, I was completely debt free and my cash flow was accelerating.

I use the following example in all my conferences and in all my books. I use it because it will help you visualize what I am saying here. Let's assume I told you I was going to give you such a powerful key to your finances that for most people, it would get them completely out of debt before the end of the year. You could see the people in my conferences get their pencils and paper out, ready to write. Then I say, "Here it is: make a net income of 5 million dollars before the year is over." There is quiet for a second, then laughing usually breaks out among the people. I will then usually stop them and ask them why they are laughing. I ask them, "Is it because that would not be enough to pay your debts off?" Then, raise it to 10 million dollars if you need to. They laugh again. Then, I ask them again, "Why are you laughing?" And then I explain, "You are laughing because you see no way you could do that, and it must be a joke."

So, then I go on and give them a hypothetical situation to ponder. Let's say that I am a wealthy exporter of fine goods, and I am desperate for help. I tell you that I have this huge shipment of balls that needs to be boxed and labeled for shipping. I also tell you that I would pay you $500 for every ball you box and label for shipping. Let's also suppose you could do 500 an hour. Let's also assume that you are going to put in 10-hour days. That means you could prepare 5,000 boxes a day for shipping. That would pay you $2.5 million per day. Let's also say that I have you sign a 10-year contract with the same pay rate. Now, when I say, "Let's make $5 million before the year is out," you would say what? "THAT IS EASY!" So, what changed? You have a plan, and you can see the outcome of that plan. All you need is the plan! When I had the plan for my company clear in my mind, I knew I was out of debt even though I wasn't at the moment.

So, how did I catch a vision for my new business? That's right. I told you that God gave me a dream in the night and directed my steps toward it.

Knowing what your harvest is defines so much of the process you need to understand before you even begin your quest for that harvest. What equipment will you need? Do you need employees or not? What licenses will be required? What are the peculiarities of that specific harvest? Of course, knowing this

KNOWING WHAT YOUR HARVEST IS DEFINES SO MUCH OF THE PROCESS YOU NEED TO UNDERSTAND BEFORE YOU EVEN BEGIN YOUR QUEST FOR THAT HARVEST.

has a lot to do with the location in which you choose to operate your business plan. If you are fishing, what kind of bait do the fish you are after go for? Your success in harvesting your answer has so much to do with the specific harvest you are after.

So, if you need money yet have no idea where to find it, you need to start at the beginning and ask Jesus for an idea, a direction, a concept. Jesus told Peter to catch a fish to pay his tax bill. Why? Because Peter knew how to fish; it was within his ability. Jesus knows you; He knows how to give you direction that will provide all the provision you need. You will still have to walk it out, but like me, once I knew that I had the right plan for me, I jumped into it with joy. It has totally changed my life, and it change will yours too.

Remember, go catch a fish! Go catch a _____?

LOCATION, LOCATION, LOCATION

We are going to continue our discussion we began in the last chapter out of Luke chapter 5 where Peter, James, and John caught so many fish that their two boats were about to sink. Remember, what Jesus said.

> *When he had finished speaking, he said to Simon, "Put out into deep water, and let down the nets for a catch."*
>
> —Luke 5:4

Jesus gave Peter the location and the method he needed to catch those fish. We talked about the nets in the last chapter, but in this chapter, I want to help you understand location. As I said, you cannot find the location of your harvest unless you know what your harvest looks like. If you cannot identify your harvest, you might be walking around it, not realizing that your answer is right in front of you. If you knew nothing about beans, let's say, and you had never seen what a bean plant looked like, how would you even know where to look for a bean plant, and how would you know when it would be time to harvest it? You wouldn't. You would just sit in your house and complain about being broke.

But again, it seems that most Christians have no idea where the money to accomplish this and that is coming from. As I said, they seem to have no understanding of how money works or how God moves money into our hands. I also made the point that when you need money, you aim your faith to hear an idea or concept that has the power to create or capture wealth.

MONEY ALWAYS FOLLOWS THE MARKETPLACE. THAT IS WHERE MONEY IS CREATED.

So again, let's be clear about this—your harvest is not money. I do not aim at money. Money always follows the marketplace. That is where money is created. If I do need a specific amount of money, I will break that amount down into the amount of business I must do to create that amount of money.

If you do not have a business, God will show you where to harvest what you need. I had a partner who had a pressing bill that he needed to pay but did not have the money for. He prayed that God would show him how to get the money. One day, he remembered a huge pile of old copper wire that was left over from old projects. He had forgotten about that pile of copper. Well, he took that copper down to the recycling center, and they gave him $1,500 for it, the exact amount that he needed to pay the bill he had.

Now, that story is a great temporary fix. Sometimes, we need them. But what I want you to build is a money machine, and that is called a business. Money comes **as a result** of your sales, the goods that can be sold, from something that is created or manufactured to be sold, or you working in a company that sells things. Remember, all money is created by buying and selling. But don't focus on the money; focus on how to create the money. Again, if you are staring at the money, you will miss the idea that will bring your harvest.

This process in the marketplace, buying and selling, is the heart of business and is your answer to poverty.

That does not mean you have to be in direct sales, but just understand that even if you sit behind a desk all day, you are in sales. Everyone is in sales.

Now, before we dig into the topic of location, I thought you might enjoy an email I received from one of my partners. It speaks of harvest and location, so let's take a look at Ken's story.

> It was 2015, and we had just moved back to Atlanta, Georgia, from Florida. Our real estate business had sort of taken a turn for the worse. We started watching Pastor

Gary on *Fixing the Money Thing* over the last couple of years, and it was very intriguing. And I said to my wife, "Let's go up to Ohio and see Faith Life Church." I felt like I just needed to know that it was real.

So, we drove up, knowing nobody, and we just came to church. We had a really great time, and as we were getting ready to leave, we met one of the greeters. And he said, "Hey, I heard you drove all the way from Atlanta just to come to church." I said, "Yep, just wanted to do it." Then he said, "Why don't you come to Kingdom class? You drove all the way from Atlanta. At least you can let us feed you." And little did we know that Pastors Gary and Drenda were teaching the class that day. They walked over and said, "We heard you drove all the way from Atlanta just to come to church." Then Pastor Gary said, "You are a businessman, aren't you?" I said, "Yes, I am." "Well, it is going to be the best year you have ever had coming up."

So fast forward to the next summer, and we felt we needed to make a change in our real estate business. We felt that we needed to change to a new broker. There was one just down the street from where we lived, so we went to their office and joined their office. It was about 45 days later that we received an email from the broker saying that they were going to close that office down. We sent the founder of the company an email saying, "We love your company, and we sure hate to see you close that office." An hour or so later, the owner called us and said, "How would you like to own the company? As of right now, I am giving it to you!" So, within 45 days of joining the company, we now owned the company. We were amazed! We then grew that company into three offices and 200 agents, and, just like pastor Gary said, it has been the best year I have ever had.

Ken went on and told me how after that great year, his wife was almost at the point of death, got down to 78 pounds, and was in extreme pain. But Ken knew the God that had given him that business was the same God who would heal his wife. And He did; she is now healthier than ever.

Ken said, "Our lifetime goal is simple. We want to demonstrate and expand the Kingdom of God. We've been there when religion did not work. We tried, and it was not working, and it seemed like things were hopeless. But we found the Kingdom, which was always here, but we just did not understand. We found out that all you need is the Kingdom. One experience with the Kingdom will change your life, your kid's life, and the generations to come."

Well spoken, Ken! Today, Ken is still in real estate and is doing fantastic. He spends a lot of his time teaching people about the Kingdom of God whenever he can. Ken did exactly what we are talking about here. He needed answers on two fronts, his business and then his wife's life-threatening medical condition. He was not one to wait around for the answers either. He came to Ohio to see if what he had heard on TV was actually true. He found out that it was true, as he met so many folks in our congregation who shared with him their own stories of the power of God. He was obedient to God and allowed God to move him to Atlanta, Georgia, which put him in a very unique place—in fact, the exact place he needed to be to inherit an established real estate brokerage with all its agents.

So, how important is location? Well, just ask Ken. When God says the fish are over there, over there is where you need to be. As an example, if I told you that I had faith to catch a 150-pound halibut from my bathtub, you would think I was crazy. Why? Because you know there are no halibut in my bathtub. You also know even if I sat there for 10 years, I was not going to catch a 150-pound halibut in that bathtub. Peter had to go to the fish. He had to go where Jesus told him the fish were located, over in the deep water. That is the key. Listen to God for the direction you need. He will tell you where you need to be.

> **WHEN GOD SAYS THE FISH ARE OVER THERE, OVER THERE IS WHERE YOU NEED TO BE.**

> **LISTEN TO GOD FOR THE DIRECTION YOU NEED. HE WILL TELL YOU WHERE YOU NEED TO BE.**

You hear this and I hear it, that when it comes to business, it is all about location, location, location! There is some merit to that, of course, as I have just indicated. But just having the right location or even the right product is still not a surefire way to succeed. As an example, have you ever seen a new business open up, and you just knew in five seconds that there was no way that business was going to make it? Then after a brief time, you saw that you were right?

It was so sad to watch what I thought was a great business idea fail in my hometown. I sure was hoping it would succeed. The owners were Christians, and they built a wonderful new building to hold their new restaurant concept. I thought at first that there was no way they could fail. They made their own fresh doughnuts every morning. They actually roasted their own coffee beans in the store as well. I mean, how much better could it get? Fresh doughnuts and fresh roasted coffee? I love coffee and doughnuts, so I was really excited about the place. The doughnuts were awesome by the way.

Drenda and I are big breakfast people. In fact, it is probably our favorite meal of the day. I usually cook breakfast myself, but usually once or twice a week, we will go out for breakfast. We have a couple of great breakfast restaurants in town. One, I would say is your typical diner; the other is a little more upscale. Both have great food. Both of these restaurants offer all of your typical breakfast menu items. But both of these two restaurants have a completely different clientele. I think in our town, people are looking for your typical egg and sausage type dishes, along with pancakes and waffles. Both restaurants have that. Then they both have a few specialty items that are unique to them. The upscale restaurant has the best cinnamon rolls that I have ever had. The diner has great omelets and biscuits. But none of them have fresh doughnuts.

And when I say doughnuts, this new restaurant made about 30 different kinds of doughnuts every day. That was a greater variety than Tim Horton's, and they were much better doughnuts as well. Also, neither of these two established restaurants have a coffee bean roaster in the front window of the store roasting coffee beans. The smell is almost worth coming in for. How could this restaurant fail? Especially in a town that has quite a crowd of older good ole boys who love to come in and have breakfast every morning. No way, I thought. But it did!

Even though I loved their doughnuts, I knew they were in for a tough time the first time I went. On my first visit, I was excited to see what they would be serving for breakfast. But to my dismay, I did not see what I normally see in breakfast restaurants. There were no omelets listed, no scrambled eggs, no sausage, or eggs benedict. There were no waffles or pancakes. Instead, they had some kind of weird breakfast bowls with some ingredients that I did not understand.

So, I went up to the counter and said, "Don't you guys have scrambled eggs?" The girl said, "Sure, we can do that for you." Can you make omelets? "We could do that." Do you have bacon? "We can do that for you." So, I placed my order, then they would call your name, and you were to go up and get your order. When I heard my name, I went up and was surprised that each item I ordered was on a separate plate. Each plate had a sticker on it stating what was on the plate. The sticker was about a one inch by one inch sticker. The plate appeal sure wasn't there. I told Drenda, "These guys are not going to make it."

I watched people come in and read the strange breakfast bowls on the menu and then leave as none of it sounded good. I could not understand why they didn't add the traditional items on the menu, but they never did. Yes, as I found out, they could make all of the traditional things people in my town liked, but they never put them on the menu. As I studied the restaurant, I saw many pictures of the owners on the mission field and found out that they had been missionaries. They were bringing some of the breakfast dishes from where they had been on the mission field. Okay, cool, that would be all right as long as they had listed other traditional breakfast items that people in my town were looking for.

I was always frustrated when I went in there because I wanted them to make it. I live in a traditional, small farming community. I knew that if they would just make a few small adjustments, they would be fine. But they never did, and sure enough, one day, they closed up. I am sure in their minds they just never saw it. They were so convinced of what they were offering that they did not understand what they were missing. I could have told them the first day I walked in. I loved their doughnuts! But the menu was not good. They were not on the mission field, so please do not serve your mission field menu here if you want to make it in business. It might have worked if we had a large ethnic group of people from the country they had been in. But our town is as midwestern as it gets. I do not think most people could even pronounce what some of the stuff on the menu was.

THEY MISSED A MAJOR KEY IN BUSINESS. IT IS NOT ABOUT YOU; IT IS ABOUT YOUR CUSTOMER.

They missed a major key in business. It is not about you; it is about your customer.

What do the fish like to eat in your area? What bait would work? I am a fisherman, and it is sometimes strange how you may be empty-handed all day, but then you switch to a different bait, and you fill your limit in a few minutes. The issue was the bait.

So, before you go and invest thousands of dollars chasing your dream, make sure you are chasing the correct dream—not yours, the dream of your customers. A good question to start with is, Do you have good food? That is simple, right? Let me say it this way.

Do you have a great product? If I was fishing for halibut, I would put a whole cod on the bait hook, not a little cod but maybe a five or ten-pound cod. That is what halibut like.

MAKE SURE YOU ARE CHASING THE CORRECT DREAM—NOT YOURS, THE DREAM OF YOUR CUSTOMERS.

So, before you even get concerned about location, or investing thousands into the latest get rich scheme, make sure your prototype is great. If you are going to sell hamburgers, make sure they are some of the greatest hamburgers you have ever had before you ever talk about investing time and money into the project. Ask all your friends what they think. Ask people you do not know what they think. Do your research. Observe how companies who are successful in your field do it. Look for stores and projects in other cities that are doing something like you want to do, and note how they do business. But before you pull the trigger on anything, be sure that if you are married, you are in agreement, and secondly, pay attention to the Holy Spirit.

In my early days of learning how the Kingdom worked, God used deer hunting to teach me and catch my attention. I will not cover those crazy stories here in detail, but, essentially, God taught me how to hunt by faith. Actually, the correct term would be he taught me how to receive by faith. He taught me how to sow a seed toward my deer harvest. I learned I could even name the type of deer that I was harvesting—just like the story I told you earlier about the young Brazilian woman in my church who harvested a seven-point buck, exactly what she had believed and confessed she would receive. Well, she learned that was possible from me. Most people laugh at me when I tell them that they have that kind of authority. But going back to my early hunting days with the Kingdom, I was so thrilled to know that when I went out, usually within 40 minutes, I would have my deer. It worked every time, and it has for the last 35 years.

But back then, when I first started, when I first moved to Ohio, God led me to this big, old maple tree that stood along a small stream. I could climb up into it easily enough and then watch for deer coming into my area. And sure enough, I had my deer in about 30 to 40 minutes that first year and again the second year that I was here in Ohio. But then Drenda and I rented a farm about a half mile down the road from the farm where this old maple tree was. The farm I rented had about 20 acres of pinewoods and hardwoods around the edges of the farm. There were deer tracks on the farm, of course.

But when that third season came around, I wanted to go back to that old maple tree, but I felt the Lord say, "No, hunt your own farm." I had a hard time with that. I knew that the old maple tree was the perfect spot, or was it? Now, I know, of course, that the perfect spot is the spot that the Lord tells you is the perfect spot. And I kept feeling that God was leading me to hunt my own farm, but I was still leaning toward that old maple tree. Now, there were deer prints on my farm, but I had not seen deer on the farm since I had rented it, except maybe just a couple. I really did not have confidence that my farm was as good compared to being up in that old maple tree.

Well, opening day came, and going against what I was feeling and what Drenda was telling me (that is a warning to all you husbands out there), I went to the old maple tree and did not see a thing all morning. I came home a little discouraged. Drenda said what you would expect her to say, "You should have hunted here; I told you." She was right, of course. I had put my confidence in my previous experience instead of following the Holy Spirit.

So that evening, I went out to the back of the farm and climbed up into a maple tree that was on my farm, and sure enough, in about 20 minutes, I had my deer. God was training me to hear His voice, and He needed to.

The enemy will change tactics against your success, and you might need to zig or zag and catch him off guard. I remember getting a letter from a partner, and he was having just tremendous success. Once he tapped into the Kingdom, things just took off. But one day, he called me and said, "Things have come to a stop; nothing is working anymore." I told him, "That is because you are on Satan's radar now." At first, you were not a threat to Satan and his kingdom with your poverty, but now, you are prospering and giving God the credit. He has caught on to what you are doing. The answer is to change tactics. Spend some time in prayer, and allow God to give you some revelation on changes that you can make. Well, he did that, and sure enough, it wasn't long until he was doing great again.

> **THE ENEMY WILL CHANGE TACTICS AGAINST YOUR SUCCESS, AND YOU MIGHT NEED TO ZIG OR ZAG AND CATCH HIM OFF GUARD.**

You see, success is not a stagnant thing. But God always knows where the fish are! So, pray about any location or strategy the Lord gives you for business; that is a must. And do not stop. You need to continually follow His leading.

> **YOU NEED TO CONTINUALLY FOLLOW HIS LEADING.**

While we are still on the topic of location, I need to tell you another story. I know you will face a similar situation in your business decisions, so listen up. Drenda and I live in Mount Vernon, Ohio. It is a great town. We rented office space for our company, Forward Financial Group, there for a few years. At the time, we had about 300 reps working for us. Most of them were part time, and many were in other states. But we had a core group of probably around 30 or so in the Columbus area. Because we lived in Mount Vernon, we had our office there. But most of our clients were coming from the Columbus area. Secondly, many of my managers lived in the Columbus area. Clients who wanted to meet in our offices found that Mount Vernon was a little far to drive.

So, Drenda and I began to consider moving our offices back to New Albany. That is where the company first started, and this was the area that the farm we rented was in. The church we pastor is also in New Albany. Additionally, we knew that New Albany was very close to the freeway system surrounding Columbus and was very accessible. But as we looked, there were no offices available in New Albany. This was before the tremendous growth that has happened there over the last 20 years. There just was nothing there, yet we really felt that we should relocate our offices back to New

Albany. And specifically, we really would have preferred an office in downtown, the old part of New Albany. After a few months, we realized that there just was nothing there and nothing that would probably be opening up soon.

We desperately needed a bigger office since we had added a mortgage company to our business model. During this transition, my lease had expired on the Mount Vernon office, so since we were looking, I did not want to resign the lease but was hoping to find new office space in New Albany. So, during this season, my mortgage reps were actually working out of my house. I have an office wing that I built onto the house for that very purpose, but it was getting a little cramped. I had a company secretary or two there plus two mortgage reps working from there every day. So, we started to give up on New Albany and started to look for a new office in Mount Vernon.

We contacted a real estate company, and we found a building that we felt would do the job and began to move toward purchasing it. We did not feel great about having to have some of the purchase price as debt, but since the new mortgage company was bringing more money in and we had been paying a lease payment on our other office, we were okay with the payment and felt we could get into the office then pay it off shortly. As we got closer to signing a contract, we felt the Lord say, "No, this isn't it."

So, we began to look again and found a better building that had just gone up for sale. We had our real estate agent look into that one. We loved it and were ready to have the contracts drawn up; but again, I did not have peace about it, and I heard the Holy Spirit saying, "No, this is not it." Well, I was not sure what was going on, but I knew the Lord had a better idea, so I told my agent I would hold off until I had some clarity on the direction I wanted to go.

A few days later, my dad called. Now, my dad was not a Christian and was very cynical concerning the things of God. In fact, I usually tried to avoid the topic and just prayed that someone else could reach him because I couldn't. Trust me, I had tried for years. As I answered the call, the first thing my dad said was, "I know you will say this is God, but your mother and I have been talking. You know that house that is next door to my pizza shop in downtown New Albany? Well, I was going to rent it out, but we have decided to give it to you for your office." I was stunned! This was a two-story house right in the middle of downtown New Albany that I could rehab into office space. I was speechless. I thanked my dad over and over again. Then, I knew why the Holy Spirit would not allow me to move forward on those other properties.

When you pray and sow your seed for direction, do not override the Holy Spirit with your own wisdom. Do not move too quickly. Give God some time to work. Pray about the location you are to go with your business.

WHEN YOU PRAY AND SOW YOUR SEED FOR DIRECTION, DO NOT OVERRIDE THE HOLY SPIRIT WITH YOUR OWN WISDOM.

Remember, Jesus told Peter where the fish were. He could not lean to his own wisdom. He already said there were no fish around. But, of course, we know he found out that, yes, there were a whole lot of fish around.

When I started in business in Tulsa, I worked out of my regional vice president's office. When I was promoted to Regional Vice President, I was expected to lease my own office. As Regional Vice President, I was responsible for training my own associates, and I also had offices that my full-time managers could work from. I thought that I had to have this really nice office to be successful.

WHEN YOU THINK YOU HAVE EXHAUSTED ALL AVAILABLE SPACE IN YOUR OFFICE OR BUSINESS SETUP, WAIT 90 DAYS BEFORE YOU CHANGE THINGS.

My office was on the fifth floor of an all-glass windowed building. The building stood on a small rise in the terrain, and the view across the city was just fantastic. But I found out that the overhead was eating up all my profit. In fact, it got to the point that I was having problems coming up with the lease money. From all that stress, I learned that overhead is not the key to making a lot of money in business. We all think that if we had the perfect location or the perfect territory, then we could win. But I found that is not true. In fact, I had a motto that I held to after that. When you think you have exhausted all available space in your office or business setup, wait 90 days before you change things. That was a safety buffer to keep me from reacting emotionally. You are always going to have good months and bad months in business. Do not react to either. Just run your race and focus on the basics, the fundamentals.

Remember, Jesus told Peter the location and the method he needed to catch the fish. He will tell you the same thing. He knows where you need to be. Follow His leading.

CHAPTER EIGHT

CATCHING FISH THE KINGDOM WAY!

Years ago, Drenda and I took a fishing trip that illustrates how faith and having the Kingdom within us can affect a situation.

We were up visiting Alaska, and as we drove along one of the beautiful bays, we noticed a number of docks with fishing boats; and often, there would be a huge, mounted halibut from that day's catch on display outside the station. Drenda had never seen such big fish in her life, and since she thought it might be something I would enjoy, she suggested we stop and go fishing on one of the boats. So, we spotted a fishing charter that had a little Christian fish symbol on its sign and pulled in. They had an opening. While I was talking to the captain and making the arrangements, Drenda was reading the bulletin board. She saw that there was a halibut derby going on that month. The prize for the winner was $150, plus their picture would be put in the local paper.

Drenda turned to the captain. "Because you're a Christian, I want your business to prosper," she said, "and I want you to be the halibut derby winner. So, I'm going to go out and catch the biggest halibut and win the derby."

The captain chuckled. Drenda said, "No, I'm serious. You're a Christian, and God wants your business to prosper. You should be blessed. So, I'm going to catch the biggest fish."

He asked her if she had ever fished before. "No, I haven't," she told him. "But I'm going to catch the biggest fish and win the derby so that you can get the business and God will get the glory."

So, he sent us out with his crew into this pristine bay. The scenery was absolutely amazing. Two volcanoes were across the bay, and one of them had smoke rising from its summit. While we were getting set up, Drenda told one of the crew members that she wanted to catch the winning halibut.

"Well, you're going to need a really big hook," he said, so instead of the size hooks he was baiting for our lines, he dug around, pulled out this giant hook, baited it with this huge pile of fish parts, and tossed it in the bay. I remember thinking, *Whatever can eat that bait will definitely be huge.*

Before long, Drenda got a nibble and reeled in a good-sized halibut. It was 40 pounds. Since you're allowed to keep two fish, Drenda put her line back out. Before long, she caught a second fish, and this one was nearly twice the size of the first—70 pounds.

"Will this win the derby?" she asked the guy. He said, "I don't think so." Drenda said, "Throw it back."

A few hours went by, and our time was up. The guy was gathering up the equipment and putting the poles up for the day. Drenda told him, "You're not taking mine yet."

So, he put everything else away, waited for a minute, then started walking toward Drenda. He said, "I am sorry, but we must start back in now before it gets dark." As he was speaking, all of a sudden, the pole dipped down. She got a strike.

"Oh, that's not a halibut," the crew member told her. "That's just a shark. I'm sure it's a shark."

"It's a halibut," Drenda said. And she started reeling it in.

It was a long, long haul to get that fish up from 300 feet down. Finally, when we could see what it was—as you may have guessed—it was a halibut. It was a big halibut. A really, really big halibut.

One of the crew members grabbed a harpoon gun to spear it so they'd be able to pull it up on the boat without the fish beating them to death. He fired but missed the shot. The fish immediately took off—and went deep fast. The reel started spinning as the line went streaming out, and it didn't stop buzzing until the fish was 300 feet down again.

I remember thinking it was going to get away. You know how sometimes you get so close to your harvest, and it looks like it's right there, then you watch it slip away?

But I heard Drenda talking to that fish. "You are not getting off my hook. You are staying there. And I am bringing you in."

So, she was straddling the pole, cranking and cranking, trying to reel this thing in. Her whole body was shaking from exertion, and I was holding on to her to try to keep her from going over the side. Finally, she got it to the surface, and one of the guys hooked it with a gaff. Three or four of us wrestled this giant fish up on the deck, and it started wildly flopping around. Two of the guys started whacking it with hammers to try to stun it while Drenda kept saying, "Don't hurt the fish!" And after we all fought with it for a while, the fish finally settled down.

So, we headed in and drove the fish downtown to put it on the town scale. They took a picture of Drenda and her fish—it was 123 pounds and as tall as she is—and later, it was published in the newspaper as her halibut was the biggest fish. She won the halibut derby, and they mailed her the $150 winner's check.

When we talked with the captain afterward, he kept saying he could not believe it. He was amazed. Drenda told him, "Faith works, you know. God wants to bless your business. You just need to exercise your faith." And we gave him some material and prayed with him before we left.

To add to Drenda's big fish story, it was about five years later when we invited a pastor friend of ours to go fishing in Alaska. Dan loved to fish; I mean he loved to fish! So, one day, I asked him if he had ever been to Alaska. He said he hadn't, but it was always a lifelong dream. All of a sudden, I just felt the Holy Spirit say, "Why don't you take him there?" So, I went over to Drenda and told her what I felt the Lord was telling me, and she agreed. I walked over to Dan and told him that I wanted to take him fishing in Alaska. He got so excited and said he would do it.

We rented an RV for a week out of Anchorage, drove down to the Kenai Peninsula, and enjoyed a couple of days of catching salmon. I asked Dan if he would like to catch halibut, and he said, "Absolutely." We wanted to go back to the same people who had taken Drenda out on the derby winning trip, but we could not remember the name of the company. But we remembered the town and thought if we could look back at their archived newspapers, just maybe, we could find the picture of Drenda and the big fish with the accompanying article, which would remind us of the name of the company we went with. Well, amazingly, we found that article online and called them.

At that time, we did not tell them who we were, but they said they had an opening. We used our friend's name to book it, because we wanted to surprise them. Their company had moved about five miles down the coast from where they had been when Drenda caught the big fish. After arriving, we walked into the office, and the couple who owned the business were there. They immediately said, "Hey, it is the halibut derby winner!" We said we almost could not find them. They answered that they had to move into shallower water as the place they had been had become so infested with sharks that they could not keep their bait on.

They said that there were no big halibut in those waters as it was much shallower. They said they usually caught 20 and sometimes 30-pound fish, but that was it. Drenda asked the owner if they had caught any large fish there that year, and he said, "No."

Then, I was shocked to hear her say, "Well, I am going to catch the biggest fish of your year today so that you will know God is for you." The captain then mocked Drenda, saying, "That is nuts. There are no big halibut in these waters." Drenda responded with, "You will see."

I pulled Drenda aside and said, "What is going on?" She said that she had talked to the wife, and the wife told her that her husband was discouraged and did not believe that God could help their business make it, as travel was not as it had been in past years. She then went on and said, "I believe God wants to encourage the owner to trust Him." "Okay," I said, "I agree with you."

Well, the story was an exact repeat of the derby winning year. It was almost dark. The captain, who was the owner, said we had to go in. At the last second, the pole dipped with a strike, and after a decent fight, a 70-pound plus halibut was in the boat. The captain was in complete shock. He said he had not seen a fish of that size in that area.

Of course, Drenda then kept telling him that it was not her but God that brought the fish, and if he would turn his heart toward God, he would find the success he was looking for. This time, instead of mocking her, he listened. He offered to take us to dinner that night, which we agreed to. At the restaurant, there were many boat captains having dinner. Amazingly, he went to all of them and told them of the big fish. All of them were amazed as they had not caught a halibut of that size the entire year. Before we left, we prayed with the owner; and this time, he was eager to hear more about the Kingdom.

This is what our lives should look like! Lives that stand out with evidence of the Kingdom. Like the captain, when others see that, they will ask, and we can then lead them to the light of the Kingdom.

That was a great story, one I have told for years. But you are not reading just to applaud and say that was a great story. No, you are reading to learn how to do the same thing Drenda did, show off the Kingdom of God.

I want to go back to the story in Luke chapter 5 that we have been looking at and let you know the real power behind that amazing catch of fish. Let's just read the story again, so we can catch a few more of the details.

> *One day as Jesus was standing by the Lake of Gennesaret, the people were crowding around him and listening to the word of God. He saw at the water's edge two boats, left there by the fishermen, who were washing their nets. He got into one of the boats, the one belonging to Simon, and asked him to put out a little from shore. Then he sat down and taught the people from the boat.*

When he had finished speaking, he said to Simon, "Put out into deep water, and let down the nets for a catch."

Simon answered, "Master, we've worked hard all night and haven't caught anything. But because you say so, I will let down the nets."

When they had done so, they caught such a large number of fish that their nets began to break. So they signaled their partners in the other boat to come and help them, and they came and filled both boats so full that they began to sink.

—Luke 5:1–7

In the last two chapters, we have focused on the fact that after they had fished all night and caught nothing, Jesus then told them where to fish and what method they needed to use to catch the fish. The result? Two boats that were so full of fish, they were almost sinking.

THIS IS THE PICTURE OF THE KINGDOM—OVERFLOWING SUCCESS AND PROVISION.

This is the picture of the Kingdom—overflowing success and provision, which stands in stark contrast to fishing all night and catching nothing.

This is your story! You are to be like Peter, James, and John as they took those fish to the market and answered questions as the crowd was gathering. All you can say is, "You just need to meet Jesus."

I said that anyone can catch fish if Jesus tells them where they are and tells them how to catch them. We talked about the nets, and we talked about the location. As we have discussed, both are critical components to a successful fishing trip. But there is one thing I need to ask you. What changed? What was the difference? What I mean is this. Tell me in detail what made the difference between

> **ANYONE CAN CATCH FISH IF JESUS TELLS THEM WHERE THEY ARE AND TELLS THEM HOW TO CATCH THEM.**

Peter's earlier fishing failure and then his amazing success. What was the difference between the two fishing trips? You must know the answer to this one if you are going to succeed in a Kingdom business. Are there clues in the story that reveal the answer to that question?

The very first thing you will probably say is the great catch of fish was because Jesus was in the boat. Well, I can agree with you to a certain extent, but we must remember that Jesus was operating from the posture of being an anointed man, not as the Son of God, as I pointed out in an earlier chapter. Let's review what happened and see if you can pick up on anything that might stand out.

The first major key that you must understand is, again, the jurisdiction issue. Something happened that was subtle but profound. When Peter allowed Jesus to use his boat to preach from, the boat—which was part of the fishing partnership between Peter, James, and John—came under the jurisdiction of Jesus's assignment. In simple terms, it had been under the partnership's legal control, but then it was willingly placed under the Kingdom of God's jurisdiction. It is critical that you understand the transfer of authority that took place. Understanding what actually happened in the spiritual realm is vital and will have a huge impact on your own business.

UNDERSTANDING WHAT ACTUALLY HAPPENED IN THE SPIRITUAL REALM IS VITAL AND WILL HAVE A HUGE IMPACT ON YOUR OWN BUSINESS.

Once Peter let Jesus borrow the boat, the boat then came under heaven's jurisdiction and Jesus's assignment. Thus, Jesus was able to receive a Word of Knowledge from the Spirit of God as to where the fish were at. A Word of Knowledge is knowledge that you previously did not know but was revealed to you by the Spirit of God. A Word of Knowledge is one of the nine gifts of the Holy Spirit given to the church. That would be you. And yes, you can receive direction and knowledge from the Spirit of God just as Jesus did. Once that Word of Knowledge was revealed and Jesus told Peter where the fish were and how to catch them, the rest was up to Peter. He knew how to fish. But there are several interesting side notes to this story that we can pick out. If you remember, the Bible said that when Jesus first came by, they had already fished all night and were washing their nets.

YOU CAN RECEIVE DIRECTION AND KNOWLEDGE FROM THE SPIRIT OF GOD JUST AS JESUS DID.

He saw at the water's edge two boats, left there by the fishermen, who were washing their nets.

—Luke 5:2

They were washing their nets. You might say, "So, why is that important?" The Bible says that their nets about broke; it did not say that their nets broke. The reason you wash and dry your nets is to keep them from rotting. In other words, God can give you direction as to where to fish and how to catch them, but only you can pull them in. What I am trying to say is your success will depend on you knowing how the Kingdom of God operates, but it will also depend on how

> **GOD CAN GIVE YOU DIRECTION AS TO WHERE TO FISH AND HOW TO CATCH THEM, BUT ONLY YOU CAN PULL THEM IN.**

well you take care of the natural side of your business. If they had not been diligent in taking care of the natural side of things, it would have been another "The big one that got away" story. The nets would have broken.

I get this question often, "Why am I not prospering?" There are a lot of reasons that could be the case, but not knowing how the Kingdom operates is probably the biggest reason. But then sometimes, the natural side of things is where the problem is.

I remember a partner emailed me that question, and I could hardly read it. It was so full of misspelled words and broken sentences that it was hard to follow. I wrote him back as honestly as I felt I could and encouraged him to work on his English and writing skills. I told him that excellence is attractive and told him some of my story of having to go through many years of hard training to better myself. Although I was called to preach at age 19, it was not until I was 40 that God said, "Now, I want you to plant a church here in New Albany, Ohio."

I think Christians like to spiritualize everything. They believe if God said it, then it must be time to launch out. No, that is usually not the case. God will usually speak to get you on a path of preparation. Look at Joseph and all the years that God had to work to train him in the things of Egypt before he could step into his destiny. So again, the point is this—your success will be a joint effort between you and God.

> **YOUR SUCCESS WILL BE A JOINT EFFORT BETWEEN YOU AND GOD.**

In review, the boat, the business, changed jurisdictions, allowing Jesus to receive a Word of Knowledge from the Spirit of God when Peter willingly placed it under His ministry. Secondly, Peter had to receive and act on that crazy word. I mean, here was a rabbi telling Peter to fish when he had just spent all night fishing with no success. Peter even balked a bit and reminded Jesus of his earlier failure, but eventually said:

"But because you say so, I will let down the nets."

Please remember what he said! That was when the grace of God was actually released into the fishing business. Putting the boat under God's jurisdiction by letting Jesus borrow it made it legal for heaven to flow, but it was when Peter said, "I will do it" that the switch was turned on. Why? Because Peter had jurisdiction over his own business, and only he could give agreement to Jesus's request to fish.

So, let's look at Drenda's story from a jurisdiction perspective. How did Drenda bring the halibut fishing trip under heaven's jurisdiction? She bought a ticket! When she bought a ticket, it gave her a legal right to go halibut fishing on that boat. Now, that in itself did not grant her a guarantee of success. It is what she did after she bought the ticket that changed things. Can you identify what she did?

Drenda turned to the captain and said, "Because you're a Christian, I want your business to prosper, and I want you to be the halibut derby winner. So, I'm going to go out and catch the biggest halibut and win the derby."

The captain chuckled. Drenda said, "No, I'm serious. You're a Christian, and God wants your business to prosper. You should be blessed. So, I'm going to catch the biggest fish."

Drenda said!

> *Truly I tell you, if anyone __says to this mountain__, 'Go, throw yourself into the sea,' and does not doubt in their heart but __believes that what they say will happen__, it will be done for them. Therefore I tell you, whatever you ask for in prayer, believe that you have received it, and it will be yours.*
>
> —Mark 11:23–24

Her faith could produce through her legal right to fish on that boat, and it would not affect anyone else's success. But she had jurisdiction over her own pole.

As a business owner, you will need to be operating with Kingdom wisdom and supernatural strategies. You should be getting Words of Knowledge about the decisions and direction you are taking in your business planning. And you need to know how to bring your business under the Kingdom of God's grace so you can see great results like Peter did. Remember, just having Jesus on board was not the key to Peter's success. It was a huge part of it, but he held the legal jurisdiction over his own business.

> **AS A BUSINESS OWNER, YOU WILL NEED TO BE OPERATING WITH KINGDOM WISDOM AND SUPERNATURAL STRATEGIES.**

We will talk more about ways to operate your Kingdom business later in the book, but first, I want to tell you a crazy story that happened to me this year. It illustrates that we must work together with the Holy Spirit to capture the harvest we are wanting. Then, we will go on to the next chapter where we will find yet another powerful law of the Kingdom hidden in the story of Luke chapter 5, a law that has the ability to propel your business at a supernatural pace. But first, a crazy story.

As you probably know, I love to hunt; and as I said earlier in the book, I have learned how to receive my deer and not hunt for them. This means the Holy Spirit and I work together to accomplish this. In 2023, I did all the usual things. I sowed my seed for an eight-point buck. Drenda and I prayed and agreed over the seed, I checked my gear, and I was ready to go. I did not hunt on opening day as things were pretty busy. I think it was around October 10th before I got out into the woods.

It was a Sunday evening, church had been great, and I thought spending some time in the woods would be a great way to relax and, of course, get my buck. I also sensed in my spirit that the buck was there. Whenever I sow for a specific size deer, before I go out, I always wait for the unction from the Spirit of God that such a deer is actually there. I had that unction. So, about an hour before dark, I went out to my stand and climbed up. Sure enough, just at sunset, an eight-point buck walked directly under my stand. I mean, he was directly under me. I aimed, took the shot, and the buck ran off. When I went down to check my arrow, I was shocked that there was no blood on the arrow. I tried to track the buck, but there was no blood trail. Yet, I knew I hit the deer; it was only 20 yards away. I was confused.

A couple of days later, I saw that buck show back up on my trail cam. I could see where I had hit him, but he seemed completely normal. I then realized what I had done. Because I was shooting straight down and the deer was directly below me, the arrow had hit a rib and deflected, leaving the buck with a slight flesh wound. Yes, I was disappointed for sure, but I learned a valuable hunting lesson: let the deer walk out a bit before you shoot. As I said, God can bring the deer, but we have to do our part.

Whenever I miss the harvest, I always resow my seed, which I did. Time went on, and we were busy, but again on a Sunday evening,

I was preparing to go out. I was in the kitchen with my camo on, ready to head out the door. Drenda was sitting in the living room as I was about to walk out. Suddenly, she said, "I really feel I have a word for you. Be prepared. The deer may show up suddenly." "Okay," I said. I assumed that meant once I got to my woods, which is about 250 yards from my house, I should slow down and be ready for the deer to show up before I got into my stand.

As I went to open the garage door and head out, Drenda spoke up again. "Be sure you have your crossbow loaded before you go out." I stopped and asked, "Is that prophetic?" "I think so," she said. Well, again, I assumed that meant I should not only have my crossbow cocked when I got to the woods but that I should also have a bolt loaded and ready to fire. As I came to the garage door that leads to the outdoors, I opened it and was shocked to see an eight-point buck standing there only 35 yards from me. Yes, I had already cocked my crossbow but had not loaded a bolt yet. I had no idea that what Drenda said was literal.

Yes, I received that Word of Knowledge, but I did not follow its instructions. I mean, really, I had never seen a buck just standing there at my door in broad daylight before. But again, I learned a lesson: listen to the Holy Spirit! And sometimes, well, many times, the Holy Spirit sounds like my wife.

I eventually harvested a young four-point buck, perfect for eating. But I will never forget that eight-point buck just standing there in perfect bow range, and all I could do was look at it. God did His part; I just did not do mine.

It is important, as a spiritual scientist, to pay attention to details. Many times, we miss keys to the Kingdom by assuming, as I did, that we understand what is happening. Assuming Drenda meant something she did not say caused me to miss harvesting that eight-point. Her instructions were very specific, but I was not listening, because I assumed too much. So, be alert and listen as the Holy Spirit gives you the details.

CHAPTER NINE

TWO ARE BETTER THAN ONE

We are going to look at Luke chapter 5 again, the story of the huge catch of fish. As I said, there is so much revelation in this one story that you really need to learn, more than I can cover completely here. But you really need to understand this next law of the Kingdom, the law of partnership. This law of the Kingdom is powerful, able to lift you higher than you could go yourself. I cannot emphasize enough how much this law will affect what you are doing in such a great way.

> *One day as Jesus was standing by the Lake of Gennesaret, the people were crowding around him and listening to the word of God. He saw at the water's edge two boats, left there by the fishermen, who were washing their nets. He got into one of the*

boats, the one belonging to Simon, and asked him to put out a little from shore. Then he sat down and taught the people from the boat.

When he had finished speaking, he said to Simon, "Put out into deep water, and let down the nets for a catch."

Simon answered, "Master, we've worked hard all night and haven't caught anything. But because you say so, I will let down the nets."

When they had done so, they caught such a large number of fish that their nets began to break. So they signaled their partners in the other boat to come and help them, and they came and filled both boats so full that they began to sink.

—Luke 5:1–7

According to the text, what were Peter, James, and John doing when Jesus walked up?

He saw at the water's edge two boats, left there by the fishermen, who were washing their nets.

They were washing their nets, which meant they were finished for the day and heading home. The text records that Jesus got into Peter's boat, then Jesus asked him to push out a little from the shore so He could teach the people better. So, when Peter was out with Jesus in his boat, where was James and John's boat? On the shore; make a note of that. We are gathering all these facts so as to better understand what I am about to show you.

When they had done so, they caught such a large number of fish that their nets began to break. So they signaled their partners in the other boat to come and help them, and they came and filled both boats so full that they began to sink.

James and John were on shore; you already noted that. When Peter had such a large catch, it says they (Jesus and Peter) asked the others to come out and help them pull the harvest of fish in. In the end, it says that James and John's boat was just as full as Peter's boat was. Both were about to sink.

Okay, stop everything. We have already acknowledged that James and John were on shore while Peter took Jesus out. But the text records that James and John ended up having as many fish as Peter did. How did that happen? This is a question you must know the answer to if you want a boatload of fish that you did not catch. It is a fact that Jesus did not tell them to cast their nets out like He did Peter. So, how did they catch just as many fish as Peter?

The answer is partnership!

I am not talking about a business partnership but rather a spiritual partnership.

> **I AM NOT TALKING ABOUT A BUSINESS PARTNERSHIP BUT RATHER A SPIRITUAL PARTNERSHIP.**

The Bible says that Peter, James, and John were partners in business; and we know that partners share equally in the expense and the profit of a business. But spiritually, something strange happened. How much faith did James and John use to harvest that boatload of fish? **None.** Stop and think about what I just said. They had the same catch as Peter, who did exercise his faith, but yet they did not use their faith for that boatload of fish.

> *So they signaled their partners in the other boat to come and help them.*

They came out **to help** Peter's faith pull in all those fish. The key here is a principle called partnership. Remember, they were all partners in the business. So, when Peter offered his boat to Jesus, he was really offering the fishing business; thus, when Peter used his faith to obey Jesus's direction to move a bit offshore so the people could hear Him better, the entire business came under the jurisdiction of the Kingdom of God. If by chance Peter, James, and John owned one thousand boats in their business, how many boats would or could have been filled up that day? Because of partnership, one thousand boats could have been filled.

Now, let's look at this story for more clues. It was Peter who heard the words of Jesus and said, "*But because you say so, I will let down the nets.*" It was Peter's words that released the power of God into that boat.

BUT BECAUSE THEY WERE PARTNERS, THEY SHARED EQUALLY IN THE HARVEST.

Here, we see one of the most powerful laws of the Kingdom of God. You see, James and John tapped into Peter's grace, his faith. But Peter tapped into Jesus's grace by obeying His word. In reality, by coming out to help, they were pulling in Peter's faith, not theirs. But because they were partners, they shared equally in the harvest. Look at what Jesus said about this principle.

> *"Anyone who welcomes you welcomes me, and anyone who welcomes me welcomes the one who sent me. Whoever welcomes a prophet as a prophet will receive a prophet's reward, and whoever welcomes a righteous person as a righteous person will receive a righteous person's reward. And if anyone gives even a cup of cold water to one of these little ones who is my disciple, truly I tell you, that person will certainly not lose their reward."*
>
> —Matthew 10:40–42

What was He saying? If you receive a prophet as a prophet, you will receive a prophet's reward. In other words, if you believe in the prophet's assignment from heaven and come alongside to support and help the prophet on their assignment, you will receive the exact reward he does for supporting him on it.

What does it mean to receive? It does not mean a simple hello and a handshake. It means if you believe in the mission of that righteous man and you help support him, help support his mission, then you will receive the same exact reward as he does.

You are partnering with his assignment, and you will get the same reward. You do not have to have great faith. You just want to help the assignment be completed, and you have come along to help make it happen.

Now, let's go over to Philippians chapter 1 where we can see this principle again.

I thank my God every time I remember you. In all my prayers for all of you, I always pray with joy because of your partnership in the gospel from the first day until now, being confident of this, that he who began a good work in you will carry it on to completion until the day of Christ Jesus.

It is right for me to feel this way about all of you, since I have you in my heart and, whether I am in chains or defending and confirming the gospel, all of you share in God's grace with me.
—Philippians 1:3–7

Why was Paul thankful for this church, and why did he have such joy over this church? He told us why, "*because of your partnership in the gospel.*" This church had been a supporter of Paul's ministry from the beginning. He then went on and said in verse seven that because of their partnership, all of those in this church shared in God's grace with him. Do you understand what he said? James and John shared in the grace Peter stepped into when the fish multiplied. It was God's grace, His power that filled up those two boats. Even though James and John did not exercise faith, but simply wanted to help, they had the same reward. Paul was saying the same thing. He was saying that all of you, the church, share in the grace that I carry.

Now, look over in chapter 4.

Yet it was good of you to share in my troubles. Moreover, as you Philippians know, in the early days of your acquaintance with the gospel, when I set out from Macedonia, not one church shared with me in the matter of giving and receiving, except you

only; for even when I was in Thessalonica, you sent me aid more than once when I was in need. Not that I desire your gifts; what I desire is that more be credited to your account. I have received full payment and have more than enough. I am amply supplied, now that I have received from Epaphroditus the gifts you sent. They are a fragrant offering, an acceptable sacrifice, pleasing to God. <u>And my God will meet all your needs according to the riches of his glory in Christ Jesus</u>.
—Philippians 4:14–19

Notice that Paul did not say, "And now, your God will supply your needs." No, he said, "And now my God will supply all your needs." Just like James and John on the seashore, they heard Peter crying out, "Come out and help us drag these fish in!" When you support a God assignment in the earth, you tap into the grace on that assignment.

Let me give you an example.

We needed more space at our church, Faith Life Church, in New Albany, Ohio. So, we began

> **WHEN YOU SUPPORT A GOD ASSIGNMENT IN THE EARTH, YOU TAP INTO THE GRACE ON THAT ASSIGNMENT.**

to raise money to add on to our current building. We are running four services a weekend, with about 2,500 to 3,000 in attendance. Things are full.

We had plans drawn up and had our builder look at them and give us a rough idea of what he thought it would cost to build based on the plans we had. He came back with a bid of $18 million. A little high, but we were planning to build the building in phases, so everything looked good. But then a few weeks later, he came back and said he made a mistake, and the actual cost to build would be closer to $36 million. Okay, stop. We couldn't afford to build a $36 million building right then. We would have to go back and redesign some of our plans.

Well, then Covid hit, and prices skyrocketed. After Covid, the builder said that the cost had then gone up to about $55 million to build that building. We knew that was not going to work, so we thought about looking for a campus site. We knew the area we wanted to be in, but as hard as we looked, we could not find any space that we liked. We continued to look for a few months, but nothing.

Meanwhile, Drenda and I were scheduled to be on the Victory TV's Victorython, their annual fundraiser. As we were sitting on the set, I heard the Holy Spirit speak to me about a campus. He said, "I want you to go home and take a $100,000 check before your people this weekend. In every service, tell them that you are sowing this $100,000 check into Victory TV for the campus we need." The Lord told me not to pay this out over a few months, to pay all of the $100,000 in one check. Now, we also gave additional funds to the network while we were there on top of the $100,000 check we were to give.

After I heard that from the Lord, I walked over to brother Kenneth Copeland and told him what God had said to me and handed him our normal check of support, not the $100,000 check but a different amount which we had planned to give before God spoke to me. He took my hand and said, "I have faith for buildings, and

I agree with you!" That was on a Friday. We went home and did what God said. At the Saturday and Sunday services, we stood up and declared we were sowing $100,000 toward our new campus.

On Monday, some of our staff went out to look at a school that had closed down in the area. They came back and told us it was amazing and would make a great campus. They said the price was too high, but it was worth looking at, even if just to get ideas. The price was $7.5 million, higher than the $4 million we were hoping for. We had planned on leasing a place for our campus at first while we saved our cash to buy later. On Tuesday morning, our daughter called and encouraged us to at least go and look at the school campus. She said it was amazing.

We weren't busy that morning, so we drove over to look at it. We were quite shocked at what it was. It was a private high school that had gone bankrupt. It appeared that the sheriff just came one day and locked the doors. Everything was still in the school, I mean everything. Gifts to the teachers were still unopened on the desks. Kids' homework assignments all laid there as if school was in session. I had to agree with our staff, the place was fabulous. A three-story school building, a workout gym, outdoor running track, five tennis courts, three other buildings. It was a fully furnished school campus! We thought, *Wow, this would be awesome.*

That night, we had a dinner planned with one of our partners. This dinner had been rescheduled three times already due to both our busy schedules. That evening as we talked to our partner, he asked how the fundraising was going for the addition. We then told him about the new estimates that put it out of range. Then, he said, "Yes, I was not feeling it. I felt you should be aiming at opening campuses." We then told him we agreed and that we had been looking. Drenda said, "Yes, today, we saw a place we would love to have, but it is too expensive." She then went on to describe all the aspects of the campus. He agreed that it did sound fabulous. He then said something that shocked us. He said, "What if I paid for it?" Drenda said, "What did you say?" He said, "What if I paid for it? What if I wrote a check for it?" We did not know what to say; we were shocked. But that is what he did. I think we were able to get the price down to $4.7 million, and our partner wrote out the check.

Since then, we have put another $2 to 3 million in the campus to rehab it. But it is awesome, and it is completely paid for. The property is now worth somewhere around $20 million. We have launched a K–12 school in the high school building, and we host 300 homeschooled students there weekly as well. Of course, our Faith Life Church campus meets there every week also.

How did that happen? I mean one day, we did not see how anything like that could happen, and then the next day, we owned a multimillion-dollar property, completely paid for.

How did that happen? The answer is partnership.

> **HOW DID THAT HAPPEN? THE ANSWER IS PARTNERSHIP.**

Let me give you an example of how partnership works.

If you walked up to me and said that you needed a car, and you have been supporting our assignment, I would say, "I have faith for cars. I will agree with you in prayer over your need for a car." Then, I would say, "And now, my God shall supply that car that you need." You see, I have to believe God for millions every year. A $30,000 car is easy for me. I passed that level of faith a long time ago.

The key to the law of partnership is that when you sow into our ministry, or anyone's ministry, you are tapping into the grace on that assignment. So, it is very important who you partner with. You want to partner with an assignment that has demonstrated results. Unless God tells you to partner with someone, you get to pick.

> **YOU WANT TO PARTNER WITH AN ASSIGNMENT THAT HAS DEMONSTRATED RESULTS.**

Kenneth Copeland had already passed the level of faith that was able to believe for a building costing millions of dollars years ago. I knew he could agree with us concerning that building. God does lead people to support projects, but you can also support faith projects that you want to partner with. Think of it as if you were looking for a partner for your business. You would look for someone that has experience in what you are doing.

Well, in the same way, many times, I will look for a ministry that has demonstrated results, one I feel that I could partner with and they could partner with me. For instance, Kenneth Copeland has given away 33 airplanes as well as given over $7 million dollars to help others buy planes. I think you would have to agree, he has faith for airplanes. Oh, by the way, he paid cash for all of them.

As a pilot, when I wanted my first airplane, a Piper Warrior, I sowed into his ministry and asked him to agree with me. He did, and through a strange twist of events, dealing with an insurance claim I had on one of my buildings, I had the money to pay cash for my Piper Warrior. That was over 20 years ago. I have also purchased a Piper Mirage, which is paid for since then. Again, he agreed with me for that plane.

> **WHEN YOU GET YOUR BUSINESS INVOLVED WITH KINGDOM BUSINESS, GOD'S GRACE GETS INVOLVED WITH YOUR BUSINESS.**

Now, you can sow out of your business account for increase and partnership. I do not tithe out of my business account. I tithe on what I take out of that account, but I sow out of that account. Just like that story in Luke chapter 5, when you get your business involved with Kingdom business, God's grace gets involved with your business. Now, tithing has not passed away, as some have said. Because the law of the tithe is so important to the success of your business, I have added an appendix on the tithe to the back of this book.

> **A KINGDOM BUSINESS IS A BUSINESS THAT PURPOSES TO HONOR GOD AND SUPPORT GOD'S WORK AROUND THE EARTH AS GOD LEADS.**

People ask me all the time, "What is a Kingdom business? Well, of course, it is a business that is operating with integrity and honesty. But basically, a Kingdom business is a business that purposes to honor God and support God's work around the earth as God leads.

And he who provides seed to the sower and bread for food will provide and multiply your seed for sowing, and will increase the harvest of your righteousness. You will be made rich in every way so that you may be generous in every way, which produces thanksgiving to God through us.

—2 Corinthians 9:10–11 (EHV)

God gives seed to the sower. That is not someone who decides to give after God has given them the resources. No, God gives seed to the sower, that person who has purposed to support God's work in the earth. To the sower, God promises to make sure that you have all you want as well and will increase your store of seed so that your godly influence will increase.

So, remember this powerful law of the Kingdom, the law of partnership. It will propel you faster and higher than you could have ever gone yourself!

CHAPTER TEN

IN CONCLUSION

It is not too late to radically transform your life through the Kingdom of God. I have hundreds and hundreds of stories of people who are now living totally transformed lives that they previously thought impossible. I told you my story of being incapacitated by debt and stress, on antidepressants, and bound by panic attacks and fear. For nine years, I lived that way until God led me to learn how He does life. The Bible has not changed. God is still doing exactly what it says. There are no dead-end streets in the Kingdom of God. Consider this story. It looked like there was no future, but God!

I was invited to speak at a pastors' conference in the Philippines several years ago. It was a long trip, and I had never been there before. I was saddened by the poverty I saw there but was excited to encourage pastors with the truth of the Kingdom of God. I started the conference off by telling the pastors my story of being in severe debt and how God spoke to me and told me the reason

I was in that mess was because I had never learned how the Kingdom of God operates. I told them many stories and lessons that I had learned about the Kingdom and how that knowledge set me completely free from debt.

I did not know this on that first day, but there was a pastor who had registered but had not shown up yet. His name was Pastor Sol, and he was in a desperate situation. He had a stroke several months earlier and had lost all mobility on one side of his body. Although he was a pastor, he had a small business pedaling a small cart through the city streets, hauling whatever people needed hauled as well as people needing transportation. This was his family's main income source. But since his stroke, he was unable to work, and his family was on the verge of starvation and eviction. Again, I knew nothing of this on the first day of the conference.

Although paralyzed on one side of his body, he was still determined to make it to the meeting. Though he had no transportation, he convinced a coconut truck to allow him to sit on top of the coconuts. He rode like that for 12 hours and finally arrived at the conference on the evening of the first day. The next day, he did not show up for the morning session. I found out later that he was in such pain from riding on that truck for 12 hours that he just could not get out of bed. But some of his friends convinced him to come to the afternoon meeting, and they promised to help him get to a seat.

Again, at this point, I knew nothing about him. At the beginning of the afternoon session, I came after everyone was already seated, so I had not seen two guys helping Pastor Sol to his seat. After I taught the session, I invited anyone who wanted prayer to come up to the front. It seemed that probably half of the pastors came forward for prayer. I was busy praying when Pastor Sol's friends brought him to the front, so I had not noticed him as his friends helped him. As I made my way down the line of pastors, I finally realized that there was a pastor that seemed to need help standing. As I laid my hands on him, the power of God knocked him to the ground.

Since I had a few more pastors to pray for, I continued down the line. But suddenly, the whole room erupted in shouting and clapping. I looked over to my left where I had just prayed for the pastor that was knocked to the ground. He was not on the ground any longer. He was jumping and shouting and waving his arms all around.

Suddenly, every pastor in the room rushed to the front and wanted to touch me. They would grab my hand and lay it on their heads. I did not know what was going on. But my interpreter told me that the guy that was jumping was the pastor who had the stroke and had arrived the night before. Pastor Sol was still shouting and jumping around as my interpreter told me that the pastors had

PASTOR SOL HAD BEEN INSTANTLY HEALED BY THE POWER OF GOD.

planned for a meeting later that evening to discuss how they could take care of his wife financially as Pastor Sol could no longer work and was paralyzed. But then, Pastor Sol had been instantly healed by the power of God, and they would no longer need to support his family as it appeared he was completely healed—and he was.

You can be sure that next day's meeting, everyone was all ears. We had a great conference, and I kept in touch with Pastor Sol for a number of years. After his healing, he started going into the prisons preaching, teaching, and praying for the sick with tremendous results. He never had any issues with paralysis again; he was completely restored.

I am just telling you this story because the power of God is still here to meet your needs. It is no harder for God to heal Pastor Sol than it is for God to give you a business idea or a direction that can bring you out of debt and effectively change your life forever. I see it all the time.

I remember speaking at one of my Provision Conferences and challenging them to think of an idea during lunch that could produce a million dollars in revenue. I remember one couple came back the next year and showed me a napkin where they had, at that lunch, written down an idea for a business that they believed could be a million-dollar idea. They went home from the conference and launched that business idea and made over one million dollars from that idea that year. They said it was not that difficult and realized all they needed to do was to ask Jesus where the fish were.

I received an email today that is typical of the letters and emails I get every day. I thought it might encourage you.

> *On May 3, 2021, Jenna was diagnosed with breast cancer as a healthy 35-year-old with no medical history or reason for it to be there. No markers, no family/genetic history. Nothing, but it*

was there all of a sudden. We were both working full time, she was a nurse, and I was in sales, and we have 4 kids who at the time were 2, 4, 6 & 7 years old.

I would describe our spiritual status at that time as that we were saved, and I was tithing for us... But Jenna was all wrapped up in the world of nursing, just after the Covid era, and I felt kind of spiritually dormant. I had heard some of your teaching, Gary, about 3 years prior, but hadn't figured out how to apply it yet, or how to tap into the Kingdom. Neither of us at that time were living in or by faith very well.

Meanwhile, shortly after the diagnosis, our daughter who was 2 was needing to get evaluated because we had noticed her speech was delayed and she was essentially nonverbal.

When the diagnosis came in on Jenna, we knew we had to fight, and honestly it woke us up. We had a couple of very close mentors really pick us up and guide us step by step, and we were given lots of great resources. But... I knew there was a different perspective that we needed, that Jenna needed.

I stumbled onto a 45-minute podcast of your daughter, Pastor Amy, talking about her story of being healed of the 13-pound tumor overnight as she slept, and she mentioned her book, Healed Overnight. I instantly went to your website and bought that book, Faith Hunt, as well as the series titled, "Live Whole"!

I can confidently say these were our primary resources to start our battle of fighting back.

Jenna probably read that book 3 times cover to cover. We shut off social media, TV, and every outside voice we could. And every night for about 2 hours, we both dug into the resources together so that both of our hearts would be in agreement at all times. We knew the Word declared that she was healed 2000 years ago at the cross, and we stood on God's promises, believing she was healed.

I increased our giving, and we started praying over our tithes & seeds together, vs. just me doing it by myself.

Since then... Jenna is 100% healed.

Our daughter found the right care through a series of events, and she is now speaking at an age-appropriate level.

Financially, we had over $80k in gifts come our way that we didn't expect or ask for, which paid all our medical expenses!

At the same time, my commissions went up at work rapidly! We had an eCommerce business on the side that started to grow again and is still growing!

But I was also led to leave my sales company, to have my own advertising company, and am now totally self-employed, succeeding beyond what we ever had done in the past.

God is Great!

As I said, there are no dead-end streets in the Kingdom of God. There is always a future. I encourage you to do what the Lord told me to do, and that is to learn how the Kingdom of God functions. You are a citizen of that great Kingdom and have legal rights.

YOU ARE A CITIZEN OF THAT GREAT KINGDOM AND HAVE LEGAL RIGHTS.

> *Consequently, you are no longer foreigners and strangers, but fellow citizens with God's people and also members of his household.*
>
> —Ephesians 2:19

But if you do not know your legal rights and how to lay ahold of them, you will live with no identity at all. Satan will try to play you like a fiddle. Don't let him! Stand your ground! You have God's authority to back you up. Do not be afraid. Although Satan subtly attempts to steal your peace and lure you into his traps, the truth will keep you free.

Let's talk briefly about the steps you would take to start a business. First of all, a business does not have to be complicated. Selling cold drinks along the sidewalk is a business (check zoning and permit requirements in your town first). Babysitting for a friend is a business. Mowing yards is a business. Think of what people need or what people hate to do, and you will find thousands of ideas for a business.

While I was in Florida recently, I had a bunch of junk that I wanted to get out of my house there. So, I looked online (hint, marketing is important) and found a listing where college students will come out to your house and haul your trash to the junkyard for a fee. The price seemed reasonable, so I hired them. They showed up with a truck and hauled my junk away. While they were loading up the truck, I started talking to them about their business model, and they said that they had over 100 locations where college students pick up junk. Incredible.

On the other hand, like in my financial services company, everyone that I hire has to go through state licensing and some intensive training to be able to work with our clients.

Let me give you a few bits of wisdom that I learned over the years.

Start by putting together a simple business plan. This is simply a list of all the expenses you anticipate having in order to run your business and to sell your product. Then, figure out how much revenue you can generate per average sale. Next, calculate how many sales you would have to make just to cover expenses. This will give you an idea if your product can produce enough income to justify the expense.

Another thing you need to decide on is the structure of your business. For instance, do you want to set up your business as a simple DBA, (Doing Business As), as an LLC, or as an S-Corp.? The very best book on the market for this discussion is Dan Pilla's *Small Business Tax Guide*. As far as keeping track of everything, you will need a software program that will track your business account's checking account. Also, I strongly recommend if you are going to hire employees that you use a payroll company to pay them. This is a must, and I would never suggest you try to do this yourself.

There are many books on the market concerning how to run a small business. I would suggest you check Amazon for some options.

Let me encourage you to open your business! Instead of looking for the money you need, create it!

> **LET ME ENCOURAGE YOU TO OPEN YOUR BUSINESS! INSTEAD OF LOOKING FOR THE MONEY YOU NEED, CREATE IT!**

Do not allow Satan to box you in financially, one of his biggest traps. You now know that you can create as much money as you need through the Kingdom of God and business. Watch out for debt, for it is a bankrupt and counterfeit system. It puts millions of people and families into slavery every day. I was enslaved to that system for years, and it almost destroyed me.

Next, study the Kingdom! Get my five-book set called "Your Financial Revolution." It will help you understand the laws of the Kingdom that God taught me and that brought me out of debt. If you have an interest in obtaining a free Get Out of Debt plan or finding out more information about safeguarding your retirement money in these crazy times, you can call my business office at 1-(888)-397-3328.

Finally, consider having us to your church or business to conduct one of our conferences in person. Call 1-(888)-397-3328 for details.

Business was my answer, and it just might be yours as well.

—Gary Keesee

A SPECIAL MESSAGE TO PASTORS AND CHURCH LEADERS

Hey, Pastors and full-time ministry leaders. Could business be part of your financial answer too? As you know, I am a pastor of a large church with 4,000 members and 4 weekend services. I also do a daily TV broadcast and do conferences all over the country. Yes, I am busy. But I do both business and ministry at the same time and have loved it for the last 30 years. This, of course, is not for everyone, but it is a great model, especially when you are starting out in ministry. Everyone is different, of course, and has different assignments. But after conducting conferences on the topic of finances in churches and meeting hundreds of pastors over the last 16 years, I found many of them are strained from the financial pressure they live under. Not only the financial pressure from building the ministry but also in their personal finances. I know personally there were some tough days in my ministry finances over the years. I think that every pastor has gone through those kinds of trials. I told my wife, Drenda, years ago that if I had to deal with the financial pressures of the church as well as having personal financial troubles, I am not sure I would have made it.

You know, it is sad that for years as a Christian, I always heard you could not preach and be in business at the same time. I have talked to pastors that when God called them, they felt they needed to get out of business and focus solely on preaching. Not because they wanted to but because they felt like they had to make a choice. They were taught that you should not do both. Now, I agree pastoring a church is a huge job, and it is a full-time job. The enemy will harass you; people will harass you; and you will face difficulties. That just comes with the job. But personally, I have loved pastoring while at the same time having a successful business.

I BELIEVE PASTORS SHOULD BE EXAMPLES TO THEIR PEOPLE. THEY SHOULD OFFER THEM A HEALTHY PICTURE OF FINANCIAL STABILITY AND SHOW A LEVEL OF PROSPERITY THAT WOULD BRING HONOR TO GOD.

In fact, I have seen too many pastors barely taking care of their families, in debt and broke. Seriously, this is wrong. I believe pastors should be examples to their people. They should offer them a healthy picture of financial stability and show a level of prosperity that would bring honor to God. They should provide anyone going into the ministry a picture of hope that they would not be required to suffer financial ruin by going in that direction. But to be honest, in most cases, it is not really the pastor's fault. Most church boards out there do not understand that they need to pay their pastors well. In fact, Paul said that they should receive a double portion.

> *The elders who direct the affairs of the church well are worthy of double honor, especially those whose work is preaching and teaching. For Scripture says, "Do not muzzle an ox while it is treading out the grain," and "The worker deserves his wages."*
> —1 Timothy 5:17–18

I think this is pretty clear. This means whatever it takes to have a good living in your town, you should pay your pastor twice that amount. The problem is we have a person on the church board who is making say $45,000 a year, and if they paid the pastor $90,000 a year, the pastor would be paid more than they make. And since a lot of people see a pastor's job as easy, they would not vote in a double portion for the pastor. But this is not their choice; it is a directive from God

GOD WANTS HIS MINISTERS NOT TO BE SO BOGGED DOWN WITH WORRY THAT THEY CANNOT OPERATE IN FAITH.

Himself. God wants His ministers not to be so bogged down with worry that they cannot operate in faith. So, if you are involved with the salary of your pastor, please adjust their income appropriately. It will bless your church as well.

People have interpreted the following verse as meaning that if you are preaching, then you cannot make any other money and should be content to live on what your ministry will pay you.

> *Don't you know that those who serve in the temple get their food from the temple, and that those who serve at the altar share in what is offered on the altar? In the same way, the Lord has commanded that those who preach the gospel should receive their living from the gospel.*
>
> —1 Corinthians 9:13–14

Is this saying that a pastor, a teacher, or any person who is ministering the Word of God should only receive the money they need to live on from those to whom they minister? No, not at all. If that was the case, Paul would be guilty as he was a tentmaker and paid his own way. Instead of taking a paycheck from this church, he said he would not take any pay from them at all so they could more easily receive the Word of God. What was Paul really saying here? Paul was teaching this young church that they were commanded to support the Gospel and those who were preaching and teaching the Word of God. In verses 7 through 11 of the same chapter, he said this:

> *"Who serves as a soldier at his own expense? Who plants a vineyard and does not eat its grapes? Who tends a flock and does not drink the milk? Do I say this merely on human authority? Doesn't the Law say the same thing? For it is written in the*

Law of Moses: 'Do not muzzle an ox while it is treading out the grain.' Is it about oxen that God is concerned?

Surely, he says this for us, doesn't he? Yes, this was written for us, because whoever plows and threshes should be able to do so in the hope of sharing in the harvest. If we have sown spiritual seed among you, is it too much if we reap a material harvest from you?"

As you can see, it is not the preachers he is correcting; it is the church. They are commanded to pay their preachers and teachers well.

GOD AND BUSINESS WORK WONDERFULLY TOGETHER.

Let me make it clear. Paul was a businessman who paid his own way as he worked among the young churches. He was a tentmaker. God and business work wonderfully together.

I have personally launched an initiative, prompted by a dream that the Lord gave me, to plant hundreds of small campuses in small towns across the United States and in other nations. We are currently working in 68 nations, establishing small churches that are pastored by bi-vocational pastors.

EVERY VISION REQUIRES PROVISION, AND BUSINESS IS THE MACHINE THAT CAN CREATE THE WEALTH TO MAKE IT HAPPEN.

Listen, almost every church needs money. Every vision

requires provision, and business is the machine that can create the wealth to make it happen.

I host an annual Provision Conference at my church where hundreds of people come to learn how to start and run a business. Every church should have some type of business mentorship program set up to help their people know how to get started and how to run a business. It can be so overwhelming. There are so many laws and regulations that many people just do not want to dive into all of that. Be a champion of small business.

I encourage my staff to have businesses on the side as long as they do my work first. Have I lost some employees doing that? Sure, but I am not their God. They are not mine to own; they are God's. If I can help raise up someone in their gifting, then God will take care of me. My job is to mentor and equip those that God sends to me.

Let's also understand that God will direct many to stay employed by the church. That is where their assignments are. As a pastor, I must make sure that I am paying them great income for their work.

I am personally pushing for a lot of bi-vocational pastors. I think a pastor of a small church can easily have a business and yet still be effective at pastoring. My goal is to raise up hundreds of small churches of around 100 people who have a bi-vocational pastor, especially in small communities. As churches, we should be promoting and teaching people how to think like business owners and train them how to run small campus churches.

Thanks for taking the time to spend a few minutes with me.

Open Your Business! It changed my life, and it can change yours as well!

—Gary Keesee

UNDERSTANDING FAITH

What is faith?

Faith is a term that Christians throw around loosely. And I am convinced that many, if not the majority, do not know what faith is, why it is needed, how to know if they are in faith, and how to find faith. If faith is the switch that healed the woman in Matthew 9:20–22, as Jesus stated, then we need to take a very close look at faith! We find our definition of faith in Romans 4:18–21. Oh, I know what you are thinking, *No, Gary. Hebrews 11:1 is our definition of faith.*

> *Faith is being sure about what we hope for, convinced about things we do not see.*
>
> —Hebrews 11:1 (EHV)

Yes, that is the traditional answer, but if you look at the Scripture, Hebrews 11:1 is telling us the benefits of faith, not what faith actually is. I believe our Scripture in Romans will give us a very clear picture of what faith actually is.

> *Against all hope, Abraham in hope believed and so became the father of many nations, just as it had been said to him, "So shall your offspring be." Without weakening in his faith, he faced the fact that his body was as good as dead—since he was about a hundred years old—and that Sarah's womb was also dead. Yet he did not waver through unbelief regarding the promise of God, but was strengthened in his faith and gave glory to God, <u>being fully persuaded</u> that God had power to do what he had promised.*
> —Romans 4:18–21

Let's understand the setting of this story. Abraham and Sarah could not have children. I do not mean they were having trouble conceiving a child and should keep trying. I mean they were almost 100 years of age, and it was over. Their bodies could not have children; it was impossible! Yet God promised Abraham a child even though in the natural it was utterly impossible. The Bible says that Abraham was fully persuaded that God had the power to do what He said, in spite of the natural facts that stated a different story.

Here then is our definition of faith: "being fully persuaded that God has the power to do what He has promised." I state it this way: **Being in agreement with heaven**, not just mentally but fully persuaded, our hearts settled and convinced totally of what God has said, in spite of the natural realm indicating something else.

Our definition of what faith is:

Faith is being fully persuaded of what God says! It is our hearts and minds being in agreement with heaven, our hearts being fully persuaded, confident, and at rest.

Why is faith needed?

Why can't God just heal everyone in the hospital when He wants to? Why can't He stop wars? Why can't He send angels to preach the Gospel to us? I am sure you have heard all of these questions before. The answer is that He can't. It is not that God does not have the ability to do so. He does not have the jurisdiction or the authority to do so. "Gary, are you saying that God cannot do whatever He wants to?" I know this sounds really strange to you right now, but let's look at the Bible to find our answer to that one.

> *But there is a place where someone has testified:*
>
> > *"What is man that you are mindful of them, a son of man that you care for them? You made them a little lower than the angels; you crowned them with glory and honor and put everything under their feet."*
>
> *In putting everything under them, God left nothing that is not subject to them. Yet at present we do not see everything subject to them.*
>
> —Hebrews 2:6–8

We can see from this Scripture that God gave man complete legal jurisdiction over the entire earth realm when he was placed here.

There was nothing that was not under his jurisdiction. He ruled over this realm with absolute jurisdiction and authority. His ability to rule with authority was backed up by the government that had set him here. In essence, he ruled with the delegated authority of the Kingdom of God. He wore the crown of that government, which represented the glory of God, the anointing, and the position of honor that he bore.

To get a good picture of what this looks like, think of a natural king. Although he is a natural man and bears no real power in his natural being, he wears a crown, which signifies he stands in representation of not only himself but also an entire kingdom and government. His words carry authority only because they are backed up by all the power and natural resources of the government and kingdom he represents.

If you think of a sheriff directing traffic, he will stop a massive tractor-trailer truck with a command, "Stop in the name of the law." Yes, the truck is much bigger than the man, and the man, in himself, is no match for the truck, but the truck stops. It stops not because of the man but because of the badge the man wears, which represents a government. In this case, the government is much bigger than the man who wears the badge. For the truck driver, there is no fear of the man, but there is a fear of the government that the man represents, causing the truck to stop.

The same is true here. Adam ruled over everything that was created in the earth realm. God's power and dominion, represented by the crown of glory and honor, gave man the assurance that his words ruled on behalf of the Kingdom of God.

It is very important to note that when Adam lost his ability to rule over the earth by committing treason against God's government, he lost his crown. The earth realm became tainted and changed. Death entered the earth realm, and Satan then had a legal claim of authority and influence in the affairs of men. It is imperative that you also understand that man is still the legal ruler over the earth realm, as God has placed him in that position, but he now has no authority to rule spiritually as he once had. Even in his fallen state, however, he is still in charge of the earth. Yes, he no longer has his crown of God's government to back him up. He has no authority to rule with God's power and glory; he has lost his position of honor. But he is still the only legal door to the earth realm. This is why God has to use Spirit-filled people to bring about His will in the lives of men.

In the same way, Satan uses demon-inspired people to affect the earth realm toward his plan for man. This principle of man's jurisdiction over the earth is vital to your understanding of Kingdom law; and once you understand it, it will answer many questions you may have in the future as to why certain things happen or why certain things did or do not happen spiritually.

You may say, "But I thought God owned the earth and the fullness thereof?" True, He does. I hope this example will help you understand what I am saying. If I leased a home that I owned to you, although I legally owned the home, I legally gave up the right to drop by anytime I wanted to. There is a clause in most leases that specifies when landlords may legally enter rented premises—for example, to deal with an emergency or to make repairs—and the amount of notice required. If I tried to enter the home outside of this agreement, it would be considered breaking and entering, even if I owned the property. If I violated the law specified in the lease, I could then be legally forced to vacate the premises even though I owned it. This illustrates why Satan had to go through Adam to gain access to the earth realm. Only Adam had the key! Satan had to go through the door, and Adam was it. If Satan tried to go around Adam, he would have legally been forced out.

> *The devil led him up to a high place and showed him in an instant all the kingdoms of the world. And he said to him, "I will give you all their authority and splendor, for it has been given to me, and I can give it to anyone I want to. So if you worship me, it will all be yours."*
>
> —Luke 4:5–7

You can see in this verse that Satan claims that the authority and splendor (wealth) of the kingdoms of men have been given to him. Who gave him this authority? The one who had it, Adam! Thus, God cannot just burst into the affairs of men without going through a legal entrance. If He did, Satan would claim foul play. No, God would have to go through the same door that Satan used to bring His government and authority to bear in the earth, and that was a man. But was there such a man?

> *The Lord had said to Abram, "Go from your country, your people and your father's household and go to the land I will show you. I will make you into a great nation, and I will bless you; I will make your name great, and you will be a blessing. I will bless those who bless you, and whoever curses you I will curse; and <u>all peoples on earth will be blessed through you</u>."*
>
> —Genesis 12:1–3

Abraham is called the father of our faith because he is the man that opened the door of the earth realm to God whereby all nations on the earth would be blessed. Of course, when this verse speaks of the nations being blessed, it is speaking of Jesus Christ, who would later make a way for the government of God to once again have legal access to the earth realm through the faith of Abraham. Abraham's faith opened a legal doorway for heaven, which God locked permanently open by making a legal agreement (covenant) with Abraham and his seed or heirs.

Let me paraphrase what I am saying. The government of heaven can only gain its access into the earth realm through a man or a woman on the earth because they have legal jurisdiction there. That legality can only be accomplished if a man or woman is totally persuaded in their heart of what God says (faith).

Another way to say it is that heaven can only legally affect a man or woman in the earth realm who desires and chooses to come under God's dominion and authority. This would be the same principle that Satan used to gain access into the earth, using Adam to do so. He convinced Adam that God could not be trusted and brought Adam's heart out of agreement with God. Consequently, Adam chose to believe Satan and rejected God's authority.

This is the same principle that God would then use to bring His government and authority back into the earth realm through Abraham. Abraham believed God, and his agreement was counted by God as righteousness, meaning that the required legal agreement was there. This agreement by both parties, God and Abraham, allowed God to put a legal contract (a covenant) in place that secured heaven's access into the earth realm, BUT it is vital to note that this agreement only affected Abraham and his heirs. A sign of this covenant was given to all of Abraham's heirs, which was circumcision. Circumcision was the cutting off of the foreskin from the male penis. As a man planted his seed in a woman, his seed had to pass through that circumcised penis, which declared to Satan and the father and mother themselves that this child stood before heaven as an heir of that legal agreement that God and Abraham had put in place.

As we read previously, however, each man or woman, although having that legal agreement <u>available</u> to them, still had to fulfill the legal requirement of their own heart being fully persuaded of what God said to actually enjoy the personal benefits of that agreement that God and Abraham made. In essence, the covenant ran the wires to their house, but they still had to turn on the switch by believing and acting on the Word of God personally.

Okay, we now know what faith is and why faith is legally required. It is now imperative that we know how to get faith and how to know if we are in faith.

How do we get faith?

Here is a clue: You can't pray for faith. Surprised? I thought so.

> *Consequently, faith comes from hearing the message, and the message is heard through the word about Christ.*
> —Romans 10:17

How does faith come by hearing the Word of God? Is that all there is to it? What is the process? Is just hearing the Word all it takes for faith to be developed in the human spirit? To understand how faith comes and what Romans 10:17 is talking about, we can look to Mark chapter 4. If you throw your Bible up in the air, it should land open to Mark chapter 4; it is that important! Jesus said in Mark 4:13 that if you did not understand what He was teaching in this chapter, you would not be able to understand any other parable in the Bible. I would say that is pretty important!

Why is this chapter so important? It is because it tells us how heaven interfaces into the earth realm, how it gains legality, and where that takes place. Nothing is more important to your life than knowing what this whole chapter is talking about. "How does the Kingdom of God operate?" you may ask. Read Mark chapter 4! In this chapter, Jesus tells us three parables regarding how faith is produced in the human spirit, which as you know now, is a requirement for heaven to legally invade Earth.

The three stories in this chapter are the Parable of the Sower, the parable of the man scattering seed, and the story of the mustard seed.

Let's begin by first looking at the second story Jesus tells in Mark chapter 4, the story of the man scattering seed.

> *He also said, "This is what the Kingdom of God is like. A man scatters seed on the ground. Night and day, whether he sleeps or gets up, the seed sprouts and grows, though he does not know how. All by itself the soil produces grain—first the stalk, then*

the head, then the full kernel in the head. As soon as the grain is ripe, he puts the sickle to it, because the harvest has come."

—Mark 4:26–29

Before we jump into this passage, let's first define our terms. What is the seed Jesus is talking about, and what is the ground? Jesus actually defines those terms in the preceding Parable of the Sower in the same chapter. The seed is the Word of God, and the ground is the heart of man or the spirit of man. So, in this parable, using Jesus's own definition of those two words, we would say that Jesus is saying a man scatters the Word of God into his own heart. Then all by itself the soil or the heart of man starts to produce faith (agreement with heaven) in the earth realm.

Before I go forward, it is critical that you remember what our definition of faith is: the heart of a man or woman firmly persuaded of what heaven says. This passage says that although the man does not know how the process works, the Word that was sown into his heart begins to grow and produce agreement all by itself. This happens if he sleeps or is awake; it does not matter, the process continues. As the man keeps the Word in his heart, slowly his heart is coming into agreement with what heaven says, and faith is being produced.

Our Scripture reference in Mark chapter 4 tells us that the heart produces agreement through a process. The story tells us that at first when our heart receives the Word, faith begins to form. Jesus compares that phase to a sprout. The sprout then goes on and continues to grow and becomes a stalk. Eventually, the head forms on the stalk, but even at this late phase, there is no fruit, no agreement, and no change in the natural realm. Then, Jesus says the process continues as the head matures and produces mature grain. When the process reaches that point, when the mature seed is in the head, agreement is there and faith is there, allowing the man or woman to harvest into the earth realm what heaven had planted in the heart of the man.

Now, pay close attention. Let's review what actually happened. Heaven sows the Word of God into the earth realm, into the heart of a man or woman where agreement is needed. At that time, the man's heart is not in agreement with heaven yet, but a process begins to take place in the heart that brings the heart, all by itself, into agreement with what was sown. Jesus uses a great illustration to show us this process. Comparing this process to a farmer sowing seed and how the plant matures, Jesus gives us a picture of what faith looks like. In the natural realm, when the seed in the head is mature, it will look **<u>EXACTLY</u>** like the seed that was sown into the ground. Let me say that again.

When the seed that is in the head of the plant matures, it will look exactly—<u>EXACTLY</u>—like the seed that was sown into the ground.

Plant a corn plant, and the mature seed in the ear will match the seed that you planted. They are the same, look the same, and taste the same. You cannot tell the difference between the two; they are identical. So let me paraphrase what Jesus is saying. When we hear the Word (Romans 10:17), we are actually scattering God's Word into our spirit men, our hearts. If we keep that Word in our hearts, it will mature; and when it is mature, the pictures in our hearts (the earth realm) will match what heaven says.

If we put it in different terms, we could say that as you sow a promise from heaven into your heart, it will slowly produce confidence of what God said all by itself. Eventually, your heart will be fully persuaded of what heaven says, and agreement will be there. For instance, if you are facing sickness, your circumstances in your body are speaking to you that you are sick. As you sow the Word of God that says that God has paid the price for your healing through what Jesus did, your heart slowly begins to become convinced of what God says all by itself.

When that word matures in your heart, the confidence that you are healed becomes what **you** believe and say. No longer are you simply quoting what heaven says. Your heart is now firmly convinced. When you say, "I am healed," it is not a formula that you are quoting; rather, this is what you believe and know to be a fact. What heaven says has now become your own perception of reality.

This is why Hebrews 11:1 (EHV) says:

> *Faith is being sure about what we hope for, being convinced about things we do not see.*

There is a supernatural assurance of what heaven says when faith is there, yet there is still another step in the process.

The man now must put in his sickle to harvest, to bring into his actual realm of existence, what he is sure of in his heart.

> *As soon as the grain is ripe, __he puts the sickle to it__, because the harvest has come.*
>
> —Mark 4:29

Notice that even though the heart is in agreement with heaven, and heaven's reality has become the man or woman's reality, no real change has yet occurred in the physical realm. Because man is the one who naturally has jurisdiction here in the earth, he is the one that must also release that authority of heaven into this realm. God cannot do it without the man or woman. I can show you this in a very familiar Scripture.

> *For with the heart one believes and is __justified__, and with the mouth one __confesses__ and is saved.*
> —Romans 10:10 (ESV)

With the heart man believes the Word, producing faith, and is justified. Justify is a legal term meaning the administration of law. So, when a man's heart is in agreement with heaven, and his heart is fully persuaded of what heaven says, he is justified. It is now legal for heaven to flow into his life, into the earth realm. But being justified alone does not release the power of God. Like a house that has the power run to the house from the power station, there is one more step—turning the switch on to release the power, and then the lights come on. Why? Because as Romans 10:10 points out, there is one more step after being justified.

A man or woman who stands before heaven and earth justified must then confess or act upon that agreement to actually release the power and anointing of God into the earth realm. Please read that Scripture again and then again until you completely understand what I am saying. This is how it works! This is how heaven gains legality in the earth realm—the heart is the interface of heaven in the earth realm, and then our words and actions are the switches that actually release heaven's power. Please pay close attention to the second part of that verse again: We are the ones that must release heaven's authority here.

The concept of heaven waiting on a man or woman to, first of all, provide legality and, secondly, jurisdiction in the earth realm can be seen through what Jesus taught in Matthew 16:19 and Matthew 18:18.

> *I will give you the keys of the kingdom of heaven; whatever you bind on earth will be bound in heaven, and whatever you loose on earth will be loosed in heaven.*
>
> —Matthew 16:19

> *Truly, I say to you, whatever you bind on earth shall be bound in heaven, and whatever you loose on earth shall be loosed in heaven.*
>
> —Matthew 18:18 (ESV)

Jesus states in Matthew 16:19 that He is going to give the church the keys (authority) of the Kingdom of heaven in the earth realm. He said that whatsoever you bind on earth, heaven will back up, and whatsoever you loose on earth, heaven will back up. Again, think of a police officer; he has the authority, but the government has the power. The police officer holds the key or the authority of the government, as he was sworn in to be an agent of that government. What he says, the government backs up. Remember, only a man or woman has legal jurisdiction here, and thus only a man or woman can give heaven legal jurisdiction here.

There is one more very important point that you need to know about faith. Let me make reference to our Scripture in Mark chapter 4 again for a moment.

> *All by itself* __*the soil produces grain*__*—first the stalk, then the head, then the full kernel in the head.*
> —Mark 4:28

Remember, Jesus defined the soil mentioned in this parable as representing the heart of man, or the spirit of man, as I mentioned before. Notice where faith is produced; does that surprise you? It is not a product of heaven, as most people believe, but it is produced here in the earth realm and is a product of your heart. You cannot pray for it or ask God for it. Faith is not needed in heaven. We will not need agreement in heaven. No, it is only required here in the earth realm, and it can only occur in the hearts of men and women on the earth. As the parable in Mark 4 teaches, there is only one way to get it—by putting the Word of God in your heart and letting the process of agreement take place. So, if I need faith, what would I do? I would scatter the Word of God into my heart and let it grow until faith was there. That is the only way it comes. Before I leave Mark 4, I want to talk about the sickle mentioned there again.

> *As soon as the grain is ripe,* __*he puts the sickle to it*__*, because the harvest has come.*
> —Mark 4:29

I believe that most of the church world has not been taught how to use the sickle, meaning they have not been taught how to harvest what they need. The church in general has been taught how to give but not how to cultivate and harvest from the seed they have sown. Jesus is very specific in this verse, saying that when the harvest of our faith is available, WE must put in the sickle. Even though we may have done a great job of releasing our seed in faith, unless we know how to put in the sickle, there will be no harvest. Quite frankly, I knew nothing about this either until the Lord began teaching me how the Kingdom operated. Let me give you a few examples of what this looks like.

I was invited to speak at a church in Atlanta. It was a Wednesday night service, and the church was not that big, but that was fine with me. I just loved teaching people about the Kingdom. As I arrived at the church, I found it strange that the doors were locked and no one was there. It was ten minutes before service was to begin. I heard a really loud truck behind me; it sounded like it had no muffler at all. As I looked over, I saw an old beat-up, broken-down pickup truck pulling in behind the alley of the church. I thought nothing of it; after all, I was in downtown Atlanta. As I waited, a man came walking from behind the building and introduced himself as the pastor. He said he was sorry for being late, but his old truck would not start. He told me he had to start the truck by coasting downhill, then once getting up some speed, popping the clutch, since the starter was inoperative. He said many times it would not start at all, and he would have to walk the five miles to the church.

As he went on telling me about his church, he told me that although he was the pastor of the church, the church's main function was to feed inner city people. They fed over 10,000 meals a month at that location.

As the pastor was speaking, I was getting upset. Here is a man of God who is feeding 10,000 people a month, and he does not even have a reliable car? He is the only picture of God that many of those people he feeds will ever see. If they see him barely making it, having to walk five miles to churh on a 100-degree summer day, what confidence would they have that God could help them? I could take care of that. I had a fairly young car with 20,000 miles on it at home that I could give him. I told him of my plan and that I would send one of my staff down to Atlanta with the car. He, of course, was thrilled. I spent that night teaching him and his small church about the Kingdom of God and how it functioned in relation to money.

When I went home, I arranged for the car to be driven to Atlanta. When my staff member came to my house to pick up the car, I knew that I was making a spiritual transaction in heaven. I knew that as I released that car into the Kingdom of God, I could believe God for a vehicle that I would have need of as well. I am not a car person, meaning I am not really into cars. Some people are, but I am not. A car is just a tool to me. I like to have a nice car, of course, but I usually drive them until they need replaced.

When my staff member stopped by, I went out into my garage, and I laid my hands on that car and said, "Father, I release this car into the work of your ministry, and as I release this car, I receive back a car...." I hesitated. I know how specific the Kingdom of God is, and I knew that just the word "car" would not do. I also knew that I had to be specific and that Drenda and I needed to be in agreement concerning the specifics of what we received. As

I stood there mid-sentence, I also realized that I had no idea what kind of car I wanted. So, I started over, "Lord, today I release this car into your ministry, and I believe that I receive a really nice car as I sow, but I will have to get back to you on the model and type when I figure that out." That was it; the car was gone. I really did not have any car in mind that I could say, "Yes, I want THAT car."

A few months went by. Of course, Drenda was in agreement with me in giving the car away, and, like me, she did not have a clue what kind of car she wanted. Over the next two months, we talked about cars, and finally one day she said, "You know, I think I would enjoy having a convertible." I told her that I agreed and said I thought that sounded fun, but what kind? Again, we did not even know what kind of convertibles were even out there.

But one day as we were driving out to lunch, my wife suddenly said, "That's it!" "What's it?" I said. "That's it," she said as she was pointing across the parking lot of the restaurant we had pulled into. "What's it?" I said. "That car, that's the car I want!" I then saw a sharp convertible across the parking lot. "Let's go see what kind it is," I said. So, we drove over to the car and pulled up behind it. Well, no wonder we liked it. It was a BMW 645Ci, a nice convertible for sure, and a very expensive one at that. To be honest with you, when I saw that make of car, I thought, "Okay, Lord, show us what to do." I knew I was not going to pay $115,000 for a new BMW, but I also knew that God can do amazing things. Drenda and I did not tell anyone about the car or mention to anyone that we were looking for a car.

About two weeks later, Drenda's brother called us and said, "I found Drenda's car!" "What do you mean you found Drenda's car?" I said. He said, "I saw this car for sale, and all of a sudden, I just felt that this was supposed to be Drenda's car; and I was supposed to tell you about it." "What kind of car is it?" I asked. "It is a BMW 645Ci, and it is perfect; I mean perfect. It is a couple of years old, low mileage, and there is not a scratch on it. It is perfect. Besides that, you know the man who is selling it." "I do?" I said. "Yes, he said; you should call him about it." Well, when he told me the car's make and model, knowing that it was the exact car that Drenda and I had said we both liked just a couple of weeks previously, I knew that God was up to something.

I called the man who owned the car. Yes, I did know him, and we talked a bit about the car, and he was telling me how great of a shape the car was in. And then he said these words to me. "You know, ever since we have been on the phone speaking about this car, I just really feel like this is supposed to be Drenda's car." I had not even mentioned to him that I was looking at the car for Drenda. The man went on and said, "I tell you what I am going to do. I am going to sell it to you for $28,000." I could hardly believe what my ears were hearing. The car was worth so much more than that. When I told Drenda about it, she was thrilled, to say the least. We paid cash for that car and still have it today. It still runs and looks great. There is still not a scratch on it, and we have taken many drives in that car with the top down, the stereo blaring, and the sun breathing life into a tired day.

Our favorite trip was driving that awesome convertible through the Colorado mountains, with our camping supplies in the trunk.

Our daughter Kirsten was with us on that trip, and I remember driving through Kansas on I-70 during the night with the top down. Kirsten was lying in the back asleep as I drove. The stars shone so brightly over our heads, and the road was vacant except for an occasional truck or two. It was one of those perfect nights where the air was just right and all was wonderful in the world. We spent the next two weeks driving through the Rockies, and I found out just how great that car handled. One word can describe it—awesome!

But here is the one-million dollar question. How did that car get here? Why was it the exact car that Drenda said, "That's it!" about? I knew that the Kingdom of God brought that car into our lives. I knew that when I sowed that car to that pastor, I was putting spiritual law into place. I remember saying that I was receiving back a car, not an SUV, not a jeep, a car; I remember saying a nice one. But Drenda and I had to put the sickle in. That car would not have shown up until we said, "That's it!" Although I was in faith when I released that car, we had not put in the sickle until Drenda said, "That's it."

Another incident happened that brought out this principle in an even greater way. As I said, I like to hunt. I live in some very good hunting country, and I am blessed to own my own hunting land. On my 60 acres, I have about 19 acres of hardwoods and about 10 acres of marsh. I hunt deer and squirrel every year with great success. There are always ducks and geese flying around, but for some reason, I never really thought about hunting them. Oh, once or twice over the years, the boys and I walked down to the marsh and jumped up a few geese for supper. But we never truly duck hunted.

Well, a few years ago, as I watched dozens and dozens of ducks flying into the marsh, I thought that I would try some duck hunting. Wow, it was so exciting! I was hooked. During that fall's duck hunting, I found out that I needed some serious practice shooting at ducks. I managed to bag a few and found that they were very good to eat as well. I noticed that many times the ducks were just out of range or on the edge of my shotgun's range, which I believed contributed to some of my misses. I was using my regular, all-around shotgun that I used for everything from rabbits to deer, a Remington model 11-87. Don't misunderstand, I love that gun, and it is a great gun. But I had heard there were new gun models that were made just for duck hunting. They were camouflaged and were chambered for three-and-a-half-inch magnum shells, which I knew would help on those long passing shots. I planned to look into one of them before the next duck season began.

Well, the duck season was over, it was then January, and I was walking through Cabela's and thought I would walk through the shotgun section to see what those guns looked like. As I walked into the shotgun section, I saw that they had a whole section just for shotguns dedicated to duck hunting. I looked at a few of them and thought about buying the one I liked, but it was $2,000 and the duck hunting season was months away. *I'll wait*, I thought to myself. But I did something unusual as I was about to leave. I really did not realize what I was doing when I did it. I just did it without thinking. I pointed at the shotgun I wanted and said out loud. "I'll have that gun, in the name of Jesus." Again, I did not think much about it; I was just making a declaration that I was going to have that gun. My heart had a clear picture of the duck gun I wanted.

I was invited to speak at a business conference a couple of weeks later, and something happened there that caught my attention. After I spoke, the owner of the company walked up and said they had wanted to get me a gift in appreciation of my coming. He said, "We knew you like to hunt, so we bought you this shotgun." I was in shock as they brought out a brand-new, Benelli, semi-automatic duck gun, the exact one I had seen in the store, the one to which I had pointed! Are you seeing this? How did that exact gun show up? I had given dozens of guns away over the years but had never put in the sickle. In other words, I had sown those guns in faith and generosity but had never put in the sickle. I had never said, "Lord, that's it! That's the one I want." But the minute I did, the harvest showed up!

I was relating the story of the shotgun to a fellow minister friend of mine. He said, "Yes, I suppose God does that sometimes. He will just bless you with a special little gift to tell you He loves you." As I thought about what he said, I realized, "No, that is not right. Yes, God loves me, but He did not just want to surprise me with a little gift." The car and the gun had come not because God just wanted to show me He loved me. He showed me He loved me when He sent Jesus for me and gave me the Kingdom!

I have said for years that the church has done a fairly great job of teaching about giving but a horrible job of teaching people how to harvest. So, can you tell what the sickle is from the preceding stories? I hope it is obvious! The sickle is our words!

> *The tongue has the power of life and death, and those who love it will eat its fruit.*
>
> —Proverb 18:21

There was a season where the church seemed to teach a lot about our confession. I have been with people, and you may have also, that would say something and then cover their mouths and say, "I need to watch my confession." That sounds like a noble task, and I agree that will help keep the Word in your heart. However, watching your confession really has nothing to do with the sickle. What? But I thought you just said the sickle was our words. Yes, I did, but just mastering the formula of saying the right thing is not the key by itself.

> Truly, I say to you, whoever **_says_** to this mountain, "Be taken up and thrown into the sea," and does not doubt in his heart, but **_believes_** that what **_he says_** will come to pass, it will be done for him.
>
> —Mark 11:23 (ESV)

Again, the sickle in Mark chapter 4 is your words! By the time Mark chapter 4 discusses the sickle, it has already discussed the process of faith and how to get it. It says when the seed is mature, you put in the sickle because the harvest has come. The harvest has come because you are in faith, agreeing with heaven in your heart. The above verse in Mark 11 bears out the same principle. Your heart believes the Word, then you speak and release heaven's authority. But notice the phrase, "_believes that what he says will come to pass._" The test of faith is if you believe what you are saying. Just saying or confessing the Word of God is not faith by itself. Unless your heart is in agreement with heaven, you can confess until you are blue in the face and nothing will happen. So, should your monitor your confession or your heart?

The good person brings what is good out of the good stored up in his heart, and the evil person brings what is evil out of the evil within. To be sure, what his mouth speaks flows from the heart.

—Luke 6:45 (EHV)

Above all else, guard your heart, for it is the wellspring of life. Put away perversity from your mouth; keep corrupt talk far from your lips.

—Proverbs 4:23–24 (BSB)

We can clearly see that what we say comes out of our hearts and what they believe. By following the process in Mark chapter 4, we know how to actually change what our hearts believe and bring them into alignment with heaven and in faith. Then when we are fully persuaded, we put the sickle in with our words and action. Got it? Great, let's move on.

As we continue our discussion on faith, I want to bring up a question that you must be able to answer.

How do I know if I am actually in faith?

That is a great question and one you **<u>must</u>** know since it is impossible to pray the prayer of faith without first being in faith. There are many ways to know if you are in faith or not, many symptoms that you need to know and to look for. You can make a lot of bad fear-based decisions when you are not in faith. Fear-based decisions will always hold you hostage to the earth curse and will cause you to miss out on what God wants for you.

So, what is the evidence of being in faith? The first sign is easy; you can look back at our definition of faith and understand that being fully persuaded in your heart is a real key. But many times, we think we are persuaded but are only agreeing in our minds with the Word and not in our hearts. You need to be able to tell the difference. When you are fully persuaded, there is, of course, a mental agreement with what the Word says but also a knowing of being sure, a confidence that brings peace and expectation.

> *Faith is being sure about what we hope for, convinced about things we do not see.*
> —Hebrews 11:1 (EHV)

If you had evidence that you had something, would you still need to be reassured that you had it? Of course not. Again, when you are in faith, there is a knowing, a peace, and a confidence that you have what the Word of God says, even though you may not see it yet. Many people say it this way: "I know that I know that I know that I know I have it." This knowing is from the inside and not from what circumstances are telling you. It is in your spirit man or your heart. Fear is gone, no more nagging thoughts of worry bombard your mind; you know it is done.

Another aspect of being in faith is joy and expectation. Your answer is here. You have it! Faith is more than a feeling of peace or confidence, although you will have that. You should also be able to defend your position spiritually. When I say that, think of a courtroom and you as the attorney cross-examining the witness. Why do you believe what you believe about your situation? How would you defend your position? There is only one answer, the Word of God.

For instance, if someone came to your house and said, "Hey, get out of my house," would you say, "Oh, I am sorry; give us a day, and we will be out"? No, you wouldn't; you would probably laugh. If the fellow said, "No, this is my house; get out or I will see you in court," your reply would be, "I will gladly see you in court!" At the hearing, you would calmly show the judge your deed. He would take one look at it and arrest the other guy for harassment and make him pay all court costs. Your confidence was established not on how you felt and your emotions but, rather, on the law and the fact that you legally owned the house.

When it comes to being in faith, I find that many times, people who do not understand what faith is are easily confused by putting their confidence in their actions instead of their only source of faith, which is the Word of God. It is easy to confuse the action or formula of acting on the Word of God with the real power of the Kingdom, which comes from a heart that is confidently persuaded. For instance, if you sowed money into the Kingdom of God, and I asked you why you believe you will receive a return on that giving, your answer should not be, "Because on such and such a date, I gave a certain amount of money." That confession is looking only at your action, the formula, and has no anchor of assurance. Your assurance can only come from the Word of God.

I cannot count the number of people I have prayed with who, when asked why they believe they will receive when I pray simply stare at me with no answer. When I ask, I am looking for their faith, their agreement with heaven. I want to hear them say, "I know I will receive because God has promised me in such and such book of the Bible and in such and such verse that it is mine." Chances are if they cannot give me a Scripture, they are not anchored and they really do not have a clue where their boat is going.

Remember, faith can only exist when you know the will of God. Why? Because faith can only exist when your heart is in agreement with the will of God. I believe that many people think they are in faith when they are not. Again, their minds may agree that the Word of God is true and good, but faith is there only when their hearts are fully persuaded. For many, their minds agree with the Word of God, but their hearts are not settled.

Here is a good illustration of what I am talking about, one which I believe will point out that many are not in faith when they think they are. What if I were to tell you that I had recently found out that the sky was not blue, as people said, but that the color blue as they called it was really the color yellow? In other words, I told you that we had been taught wrong all our lives about colors and that blue is not really blue but yellow. What would you do? Would you gasp in shock and quickly grab your cell phone and call your first-grade teacher and yell at them, accusing them of messing up your life, teaching you all the colors wrong? I do not think so. There would be no emotional reaction of fear, no drama.

You would simply know that I was an idiot, dismiss the comment as irrational, and go about your business. Why? Because you are fully persuaded that blue is blue!

Now, let's compare my example to our faith discussion. What if you were fully persuaded of what God said about healing, and a doctor told you that you were going to die of cancer? You would look at that doctor and think he was the idiot because you knew there was no way that could happen. Why? It's because you were fully persuaded of the healing provisions that Jesus paid for. Do you see it? Of course, many people pray, but upon examination, I find their prayers are not prayers of faith but of hope, with them unsure of the outcome. My friend, this is why it is so important that we build ourselves up with the Word of God. We need to know what God's will is so that we can be confident in what He says, and also so we can reject what is not His will. Let me give you an example from my own life which illustrates just how important it is to feed on what God says about life.

I was tired, as it had been a tough few weeks as a business owner (this was before I pastored a church). My schedule had been packed with sales calls and, of course, the financial pressure of living on commissions. I was going to my dentist for a routine filling. Everything was normal until the dentist went to inject the Novocain. As he inserted the needle, there was a sudden jolt, and then my jaw instantly went numb, as opposed to it slowly numbing up. I was surprised, and I told the dentist what had happened. He said, "Oh, I guess I hit the nerve." I quickly asked him, "Is that normal?" He said these words, "Well, it usually heals up." What? Did I hear him correctly? "Doctor, what do you mean it usually heals up?" He said, "Well, about 80 percent to 85 percent of the time, it completely heals up with no permanent negative effect."

What? Suddenly, fear rose up in me. Now what? Is it going to heal up? My mind was starting to be consumed with fearful thoughts. After my appointment, my face stayed numb, unlike a normal dentist's appointment where the numbness slowly wears off. I was heading to a client's appointment about an hour away from the dentist's appointment, so I had plenty of time to think about what had just happened. But all the way to that appointment, I was in agony, not from any pain but from the lack of peace and from the fear that was swirling through my mind.

On the way home from the appointment, later in the day, I stopped at a friend's house. My face was still numb, and I was looking for some reassurance from someone that this thing would heal up. Notice my mistake: I did not look to the Word of God for my confidence but to a person who was not even a strong believer. I told this person what had happened and was waiting for their, "That's no big deal, Gary; it will heal up!" Instead, here is what I heard. "Oh, no! I had a friend who had that happen, and their face never healed. Their face has been paralyzed ever since." I could not believe what I was hearing! My mind was then in fear overdrive. I acted like I knew it would be okay and thanked him for his time.

In desperation, I stopped by another friend's home and asked the same question, and in shock, I heard the same reply, "Oh, no," they said, "I had a friend who had this happen, and their face never healed. Their face is still paralyzed today."

After this visit, I was undone. I knew that God heals (in my mind), but I just could not get rid of that fear. My heart was definitely not persuaded. That night, I was in agony! My mind was full of fear, and my face was still just as numb as it had been at the dentist's office. As I was trying to get to sleep, I began to feel a bit of pain under my right ear. Could it be? My dad had fought a battle with Bell's palsy a year or two earlier, and he had told me that it had started with some pain just under his ear. Bell's palsy occurs when the nerve that controls the facial muscles, which travels through a small hole in the bone just under the ear, becomes pinched by an infection or inflammation.

As I lay there trying to find sleep, all I could hear were these words going through my thoughts, "You are going to have Bell's palsy just like your dad." When I woke up in the morning, I had a full-blown case of Bell's palsy! Not only was my jaw numb, but also my entire face on the right side was numb as well, and I could not close my eyes or my mouth. I was a mess.

I went to a local doctor to confirm my suspicions. After the examination, he looked at me and said that I indeed had a full- blown case of Bell's palsy. I then said, "What happens next?" He said, "Well, in about 80 to 85 percent of the cases, it will heal up without permanent paralysis." "Did he say what I thought he just said?"

At that point, I knew that I was in trouble. I knew that the devil would not stop there, and I did not want to see what came next. I knew enough about spiritual warfare to realize I was heading in the wrong direction. Remember, this was years ago before I knew very much about these types of things. But I knew enough to realize that I had to tackle this thing spiritually if I was going to have any success at beating it. I also realized that this was a demonic setup to catch me off guard when I was tired and not anticipating any trouble.

At that point, I knew that my only hope was the Word of God. In myself, I had absolutely no ability to stop the fear that was plaguing my mind. So, I wrote out 3 x 5 cards with healing Scriptures on them and posted them all over my house. I repented before the Lord and began the process of developing faith in my heart. I knew that I had to sow the Word in my heart for faith to develop, so I would meditate on the Word of God throughout the day.

At first, nothing changed. My face stayed numb, and I constantly fought the spirit of fear. After about a week, with still nothing changing in my face, it happened!

Just like the process our Scripture in Mark 4:26–28 teaches, as I sowed the Word into my heart, faith began to be formed, first the blade, then the stalk, the head, and then the mature grain in the head.

Throughout this entire process, there was not agreement and thus no faith—yet. However, even though I did not see change or know how this process works, according to our Scripture in Mark 4, things were indeed changing.

The change I am talking about is not in the manifested natural realm yet, but the change is occurring in our hearts. If we hold on to the Word, the Word slowly changes our hearts' belief system from one of unbelief to agreement with heaven all by itself.

So, in this case, I held on to the Word, knowing that it was my only answer. Suddenly, one day, as I was walking through my house with all those 3 x 5 cards with healing Scriptures on them posted everywhere, I just happened to glance at one that I had seen a hundred times. But this time when I looked at it, BAM!

Suddenly, the anointing came on me, fear instantly left, and I KNEW that I was healed. Yes, my face was still numb. There was no change, but I knew I was healed. Within a couple of hours, my face was completely normal, with all the numbness gone. Praise God! The Word works!

Even though I had allowed my spiritual life to weaken due to my neglect and busyness, I eventually realized my mistake and repented from my foolishness. This was way back when I was first learning how faith really worked, and I did not have a lot of experience in this area. I look back on what I did, asking people of my future when in trouble instead of going straight to the Word of God, as foolish. Once I understood what was going on, I did turn to the Word of God with confidence. Unfortunately, most people are not confident in this process because they have never been taught about faith and how it comes. Since they are unaware of the process, when they are under pressure, they let go of the Word, thinking it does not work.

Understand Satan's counterattack

Christine came to our church not knowing much about God. She was born again in one of our Sunday morning services, and her life was radically changed. In our church, we have a Kingdom orientation class. One of the areas we talk and teach about is the legal right to receive healing. Christine had been having trouble with her hearing for years. In fact, she had been wearing a hearing aid for 40 years and had already lost over 50 percent of her hearing. Her mother was deaf, and her brother was also suffering from this same issue with loss of hearing. When Christine heard that, as a believer, she had a legal right to be healed, she was so excited!

In the class, my wife, Drenda, laid her hands on her and prayed for her hearing to be open, and instantly, pop, she could hear perfectly. Christine began screaming and crying and praising God. When Drenda and Christine came and told me the good news, I felt an urge to warn her about Satan's counterattack. I told Drenda to instruct Christine that if the symptoms started to come back for her to speak boldly to the issue and declare that she was healed and for Satan to back off. The next morning, the test came. Her hearing had reverted back to her inability to hear well. So, she did exactly what we said, "NO! Satan, I am not receiving this. I am healed, and I was healed, in the name of Jesus!" Pop! Her ears popped opened, and they have stayed open ever since.

Remember that Satan will counterattack and try to retake territory. Don't let him do it. Stand on the Word of God!

In this appendix, I have taken some time to give you a basic understanding of what faith is, how it functions, how to know if you are in faith, and where to get faith. For the Kingdom of God to operate in your life, you have to know this. Remember, Jesus told the woman that received her healing in Matthew 9:20–22, "Your faith has healed you." And so shall it be for you: Your faith, your heart being fully convinced of what heaven says, and putting in the sickle will be your answer for any problem or need you may face in life.[8]

---

8 The teaching in the Faith Appendix was taken from my *Your Financial Revolution*: The Power of Allegiance book.

THE MYSTERY OF THE TITHE

I frequently receive emails from people trying to convince me that this law of the Kingdom—the tithe—has passed away and is no longer valid.

However, I have found this Kingdom principle so important that I have dedicated an entire appendix to it.

I know that you, if you have been around church life at all, have heard of the tithe. But I also know that what you have heard is probably not completely accurate, and it is important that we straighten out some of the old religious mindsets about the tithe before we continue.

First of all, if you do not know, the word tithe actually means a tenth. The word was used to describe to God's people the amount of their income they were to give to His work, a tenth, or a tithe.

Now, this explanation of the tithe is in very simple terms, and I want to dig much deeper into this topic in this appendix. But for now, if this concept is new to you, this is basically what the tithe is, giving a tenth to God.

Secondly, when most people think of the tithe, they also think of the Old Testament and the Law of Moses where the tithe was required in the nation of Israel for all citizens.

Today, there is much confusion in the body of Christ around the tithe, what it is, and whether it is still in effect or passed away with the coming of Jesus.

As I shared earlier,, when God told me to learn all I could about how His Kingdom operated, I really became a spiritual scientist. I wanted to know how everything worked, and the tithe was a big question that I had to answer.

So let's take a look at the tithe, where it came from, what it does, and why it is for today.

Although we actually see the tithe very prominently in the Law of Moses as a written requirement, the tithe did not begin with the Law of Moses. To find its origin, we need to go back to the beginning and the lives of Adam and Eve.

As mentioned previously, <u>Adam was created and set in the earth as the ruler over the earth on behalf of the Kingdom of God.</u>

> *You made them a little lower than the angels; you crowned them with glory and honor and put everything under their feet. In putting everything under them, God left nothing that is not subject to them.*
>
> —Hebrews 2:7–8a

Adam was crowned with glory and honor, and there was nothing on the earth that was not subject to him. The term *crowned* gives us a great picture of how this functioned.

If you look at a natural king, he wears a crown, and, although he's just a man, the crown indicates that the entire government backs up his words. So it was with Adam. He ruled the earth with complete authority, with heaven backing up all that he did. We must remember that in himself, he was just a man and ruled only through delegated authority. He had the glory (power) and the honor (position and authority) of the Kingdom of God backing him up.

Interestingly, we see Satan already on the earth when Adam was created, as he had been cast down to the earth before the creation of man. Satan despised this lowly creature (in the natural) that ruled over him on behalf of the Kingdom of God. He wanted to find a way to take that authority from Adam, basically to nullify Adam's authority to rule.

Of course, Satan had no power to undermine or overthrow Adam's position, so he had to devise a plan to deceive Eve into believing that God could not be trusted and that she and Adam should rebel against God and follow him.

Satan's plan was successful. Adam and Eve rebelled against God and lost their places of authority. At that moment, since the entire earth realm was under Adam's dominion, Adam basically kicked God out of the earth as far as God's spiritual authority was concerned, and man was separated from God.

Much happened spiritually at that moment, but I do not have time to cover it here as I want to focus on our topic of the tithe. So, let's go back to that moment when Adam and Eve fell and find out what happened.

> *To Adam he said, "Because you listened to your wife and ate fruit from the tree about which I commanded you, 'You must not eat from it,' cursed is the ground because of you; through painful toil you will eat food from it all the days of your life. It will produce thorns and thistles for you, and you will eat the plants of the field. By the sweat of your brow you will eat your food until you return to the ground, since from it you were taken; for dust you are and to dust you will return."*
>
> —Genesis 3:17–19

In a quick glance, we see that man lost his provision (was kicked out of the garden), his purpose then became survival, and he was to survive by his own painful toil and sweat. God also told him that he would return to the ground, that he would *die* someday.

The concepts of death and painful survival were totally foreign to Adam, and fear and hopelessness entered the world.

As you can see, and as Adam found out, the world had drastically changed.

I now want to go to Luke 4 where we will find another very important change that took place.

> *The devil led him up to a high place and showed him in an instant all the kingdoms of the world. And he said to him, "I will give you all their authority and splendor; it has been given to me, and I can give it to anyone I want to. If you worship me, it will all be yours."*
>
> —Luke 4:5–7

In this passage, Satan claims that all the money pertaining to the kingdoms of the earth (nations) is under his jurisdiction and states that this authority was given to him. And in that statement he is correct, as it was Adam who gave this authority to him in his rebellion.

Notice this verse says that all the splendor of the nations or kingdoms of the world were now under his jurisdiction. What is the splendor of a nation? Its *wealth*.

All the money in the earth realm has a kingdom, a nation, stamped on it, so all money is part of or under the jurisdiction of an earthly kingdom. Satan now claims that the money, or the wealth, of the nations are under his jurisdiction, and he claims he can give it to whomever he wants. To put it simply, Satan claims jurisdiction over the wealth and prosperity of the nations. This is very important as we will find out that the tithe has a very specific purpose tied to that fact.

> *Adam made love to his wife Eve, and she became pregnant and gave birth to Cain. She said, "With the help of the Lord I have brought forth a man." Later she gave birth to his brother Abel.*
>
> *Now Abel kept flocks, and Cain worked the soil. In the course of time Cain brought <u>some</u> of the fruits of the soil as an offering to the Lord. And Abel also brought an offering—<u>fat portions from some of the firstborn of his flock</u>. The Lord looked with favor on Abel and his offering, but on Cain and his offering he did not look with favor. So Cain was very angry, and his face was downcast.*
>
> *Then the Lord said to Cain, "Why are you angry? Why is your face downcast? <u>If you do what is right</u>, will you not be accepted? But if you do not do what is right, sin is crouching at your door; it desires to have you, but you must rule over it."*
>
> —Genesis 4:1–7

Okay, what was going on there? This was the first generation of kids. Why were they giving an offering? There was no written law stating to do so at that time, so why were they doing it?

We can assume that Adam and Eve, their parents, *taught* them to give offerings. We also can assume that God does not do things just for the ritual of doing them and there had to be a *legal* reason why Adam and Eve were taught to give offerings.

If you look at the text, you will see that there was a big difference in what the two boys brought to offer. Now, do not get hung up with what they had to offer, one offering animals and the other one offering plants, because that was not the issue. The issue was *how* they were offering what they had and why they were doing it in the first place.

Notice that Cain gave "some" of the fruit of the soil. But Abel brought the "fat portions from some of the firstborn" of his flock. Do you see the difference? In one case, it was "some" compared to the "best portion," which was the fat portion from the firstborn of the flock.

Why would Abel bring the fat portion, and why from the firstborn?

God must have told Adam the requirements for this offering.

Do you see it? This was the first time the tithe was seen.

If you study the tithe in the Law of Moses, it was always the **first** 10% given from **the best**. In this story, we can clearly see that Abel was giving the tithe, the *first* and the *best*. However, Cain was not happy to be giving up *some* of his crop and to have to honor God, and decided to bring "some" of his crops, not the first or the best.

Apparently, Cain knew what to offer and how to offer the tithe to the Lord as God said to him, "*If you do what is right, will you not be accepted? But if you do not do what is right, sin is crouching at your door; it desires to have you, but you must rule over it.*"

But Cain rejected God's encouragement to do what he had been taught and instead killed Abel, his brother. Possibly, he may have thought that with Abel out of the way, he could control both the field and the livestock, or his greed tempted him to bring only some of the crop, going through the motions of obedience with his heart far from God. I am only guessing. One thing we do know is that Cain did not want to tithe as he was taught.

At this point, you may be asking, "Why the tithe in the first place? Why did God require them to tithe?" I will answer those questions, but first, let's see what else we can learn about the tithe before we jump into those questions.

The next time we see the tithe show up is the first time the word *tithe* is actually used.

> *After Abram returned from defeating Kedorlaomer and the kings allied with him, the king of Sodom came out to meet him in the Valley of Shaveh (that is, the King's Valley). Then Melchizedek king of Salem brought out bread and wine. He was priest of God Most High, and he blessed Abram, saying, "Blessed be Abram by God Most High, Creator of heaven and earth. And praise be to God Most High, who delivered your enemies into your hand." Then Abram gave him a tenth of everything.*
>
> —Genesis 14:17–20

The question we need to ask here is: How did Abraham know to tithe and why?

Obviously, the tithe was passed down through the generations from Adam's time. And we know that the tithe was taught to Adam by God Himself after the rebellion. Here we see the actual word tithe used, indicating a tenth was given.

Many people will say that the tithe was part of the Law of Moses, meaning that the New Testament believer is not under the need to tithe. The two incidents I have mentioned, Cain and Abel and then Abraham, prove that the tithe was given *before* the Law of Moses was written. Oh, I agree, the tithe was written into the Law of Moses, and the nation of Israel was required to tithe. But the tithe was something that the nation was already doing when Moses came on the scene.

So why was the tithe written into the Law of Moses? When the Law of Moses was written, it was to govern the entire life of the new nation of Israel that had just come out of Egypt. All of the legal and governing requirements were being set in its written code of conduct by which the people would live. Thus, the tithe was written into the Law of Moses to ensure it was being done as part of the life of the nation. The tithe was so important that God had it written into the law of the nation. We will find out why God wanted to make sure it was being done in a minute, but let's look at a few more examples of the tithe.

> *Now this is what the Lord Almighty says: "Give careful thought to your ways. You have planted much, but harvested little. You eat, but never have enough. You drink, but never have your fill. You put on clothes, but are not warm. You earn wages, only to put them in a purse with holes in it."*

This is what the Lord Almighty says: "Give careful thought to your ways. Go up into the mountains and bring down timber and build my house, so that I may take pleasure in it and be honored," says the Lord. "You expected much, but see, it turned out to be little. What you brought home, I blew away. Why?" declares the Lord Almighty. "Because of my house, which remains a ruin, while each of you is busy with your own house. Therefore, because of you the heavens have withheld their dew and the earth its crops. I called for a drought on the fields and the mountains, on the grain, the new wine, the olive oil and everything else the ground produces, on people and livestock, and on all the labor of your hands."

—Haggai 1:5–11

In this passage, the prophet Haggai is rebuking the nation of Israel for not rebuilding the temple once they returned from exile in Babylon. They are not prospering, they are in lack, the crops are not good, and the whole nation is suffering. God tells the nation to give careful thought to **their ways**, implying that there was something they were doing or not doing that was causing the lack.

God says, "***Because of you*** *the heavens have withheld their dew.*" He says He had to call for the drought because of what **they** were doing. They were all building their own homes and yet leaving God's temple in ruins. This indicates that they were not tithing.

See, the tithe was to be brought to the Levites—the priests—and used for the temple ministry. Since the tithe was not being brought to the Levites, and the temple was not being built, God had to withdraw His hand of blessing because of what they were doing.

Make sure that you understand it was not God's will that He withdraw His blessing from the nation of Israel. He had no choice, as it was a legal issue involving the tithe.

As we continue to read in chapter two, we see that, apparently, the people began to heed the prophet's words.

> *"Now give careful thought to this from this day on—consider how things were before one stone was laid on another in the Lord's temple. When anyone came to a heap of twenty measures, there were only ten. When anyone went to a wine vat to draw fifty measures, there were only twenty. I struck all the work of your hands with blight, mildew and hail, yet you did not return to me," declares the Lord. "From this day on, from this twenty-fourth day of the ninth month, give careful thought to the day when the foundation of the Lord's temple was laid. Give careful thought: Is there yet any seed left in the barn? Until now, the vine and the fig tree, the pomegranate and the olive tree have not borne fruit. From this day on I will bless you."*
>
> —Haggai 2:15–19

Since they put the temple first again, God told them to mark the day and the hour because they were going to see a dramatic increase in their prosperity. He wanted them to mark the spot to encourage and motivate them to remember the change so they would not stop tithing again, not for His benefit but for their own.

There are some real keys here that will make sense in a minute, but the first thing I want you to realize is that the tithe is a *legal* issue.

God *had* to withdraw His hand when they weren't tithing, not because He *wanted* to but because He *had* to.

> *"For I am the Lord, I do not change; therefore you are not consumed, O sons of Jacob. Yet from the days of your fathers you have gone away from My ordinances and have not kept them. Return to Me, and I will return to you," says the Lord of hosts.*
>
> *"But you said, 'In what way shall we return?'*
>
> *Will a man rob God? Yet you have robbed Me!*
>
> *But you say, 'In what way have we robbed You?'*
>
> *In tithes and offerings. You are cursed with a curse, for you have robbed Me, even this whole nation. Bring all the tithes into the storehouse, that there may be food in My house, and try Me now in this," says the Lord of hosts, "If I will not open for you the windows of heaven and pour out for you such blessing that there will not be room enough to receive it. And I will rebuke the devourer for your sakes, so that he will not destroy the fruit of your ground, nor shall the vine fail to bear fruit for you in the field," says the Lord of hosts; "and all nations will call you blessed, for you will be a delightful land," says the Lord of hosts.*
>
> —Malachi 3:6–12 (NKJV)

Here we see a different prophet rebuking the nation, stating that they are robbing God of His ability to bless His people. He says they—the whole nation—are under a curse because of what they are *not* doing. They are instructed to bring the whole tithe into the storehouse, that there may be food in God's house.

Again, the tithe was to be brought to the Levites, the priests. The people were bringing some but not the whole tithe (remember Cain's sin). The Lord is telling the people that if they will bring the whole tithe that the blessing of heaven will be theirs again. Heaven will have legal jurisdiction to move in their midst. God tells them that if they will return to Him with the tithe, then they will have such blessing they will not be able to contain it.

Okay, let's stop here and talk about this for a minute before I go any further.

So far, we have seen that the tithe was started clear back in the beginning, and now we can see why. Here we see the tithe gives God legal jurisdiction to step in between the devourer, Satan, and God's people and to rebuke Satan.

Basically, God was saying, "Hands off, Satan! You cannot touch their stuff!"

See, when Adam fell, Satan would have just loved to completely starve him off the planet. But, immediately, God put the tithe in place to protect Adam and Eve. When Adam and Eve chose to tithe, they were putting God first. They were choosing God.

Let's remember that Satan gained his entrance into the earth realm in the same manner. By convincing Adam and Eve to believe him instead of God, he gained legal entrance. So by tithing—giving

God 10% of what they had—it gave God the legal right to protect Adam and Eve's provision.

We need to remember that the tithe was a law that pertained only to man's provision on the earth in Satan's territory. It did not change their status in regard to bringing spiritual restoration. No, a sacrifice for sin would have to be made first before that could happen. But the tithe did allow God to stop Satan from stealing provision from them, and it would allow them to survive on the earth.

Many people say that the tithe was an Old Testament law and has now passed away, being fulfilled by Jesus's sacrifice. But we have seen that the law of the tithe was put in place clear back at the fall of man before the Law of Moses was written.

The tithe was put in place to act as a legal fence around Adam and Eve then, and it still acts as a legal shield around us today.

The tithe is a law of the earth realm and remains in force as long as Satan is loose on the earth, as he currently is. As long as Satan is here, the law of the tithe is still in effect.

Another thing you may see in church are people who are tithing and yet not prospering. This is because of some wrong teaching in regard to the tithe. People think if they just tithe, the blessing of the Lord will cause them to enjoy overflowing prosperity, more than they could contain. When they begin to tithe and don't see their prosperity overflowing, they conclude that the tithe does not work. But their assumption is not accurate, and we need to take a closer look at the text to find out why.

God told the people that if they tithed, "*I will prevent pests from devouring **your crops**, and the **vines in your fields** will not drop their fruit before it is ripe.*"

Do you see it? It says that the windows of heaven will be opened and God will bless *their* crops. The point I am making is that *you* still have to grow something inside the fence of the tithe.

The tithe by itself does not cause you to prosper. It only protects what you do inside of the fence, the tithe.

So if you have three tomato plants, they are going to prosper. But if all you have are three tomato plants, you will have three great plants, but you will not be prospering very much.

It is what *you* build or grow inside the fence that causes you to overflow with abundance.

Sadly, with wrong teaching, many of God's people tithe and then sit down with an iced tea and wait for the abundant overflow to begin. The overflow will begin when we understand our part in the process.

So again, let's review.

1. The tithe came into the earth at the beginning, at the fall of man.
2. It was written into the Law of Moses because the Law of Moses dictated how the nation of Israel lived. God, wanting to be sure He could bless them, wrote it into that law to ensure it continued. The law of the tithe has not passed away. But the legal requirement to tithe has. Now, we have the *choice* to tithe and take advantage of its benefit.
3. The law of the tithe is a law of the earth realm and will remain as long as Satan is on the loose.
4. The tithe does not automatically cause you to prosper, but it does allow God to stop Satan from interfering with what you are growing or building inside the fence of the tithe.
5. The tithe has no bearing on if you go to heaven or not. You will go to heaven if you call on the name of Jesus. But the tithe will affect your prosperity here on the earth.
6. The tithe belongs to God's storehouse. In the Old Testament, it fed and took care of the priests who worked in the ministry. It is no different today. The tithe should be given to your home church. God has ordained the tithe to take care of the ministry.

I have people tell me they don't like their church and ask if they have to tithe there. My answer? Find a new church, one that teaches faith and the Kingdom.

If you are in between churches, you can tithe to a ministry that you are feeding from, but being in a good home church is God's best. If there are none in your area, then you can tithe, again, to where you are being fed.

7. You cannot name your tithe. For instance, as you sow your tithe, you can't say, "I am planting my tithe as a seed for _____." The tithe already has its assignment. You can name an offering but not the tithe.

8. The tithe is 10% of what you make. This is *before* taxes. Remember, God said through Malachi, "Bring *all* the tithe into the storehouse." Nine percent is not the tithe. Six percent is not the tithe. The tithe is 10%. If you say, "I cannot afford to pay that 10%," do what God was telling Israel to do when they were not bringing the whole tithe: "Test me in this," He said. Give your tithe by faith, knowing that God will honor it.

9. How do I know what to tithe on? My rule of thumb is this: Is it taxable income?

10. If it is taxable income, then I tithe on it. Does my business tithe? Again, is it taxable? I do not pay a tithe on the gross income of my business. I sow from my business as I want to, but that is not the tithe. If I pull money out of my business, then I tithe on what I take out of the business when I take it out of the business.

11. What if I do not have a church at the moment? You can tithe to whoever is feeding you spiritually until you find a church. Yes, many people do consider a distant church as their primary church through modern livestream and Facebook live broadcasts. If there is not a good Bible believing church in your town, you can tithe to a distant church. Many people in rural areas have made faithlifechurch.org their home church because of that very thing.

Okay, let's move on.

The Lord showed me that most Christians give their tithe as a bill they owe (if they even tithe, and most do not). This means they exercise no faith in what they are doing but just know they owe the tithe and simply pay it as they would a bill.

While it is good to pay your tithe, you always want to pay your tithe in faith. Otherwise, your giving is being prompted from a legal standpoint instead of a faith-based viewpoint.

Let every word of God be revelation to you of God's intent toward you. The tithe is not a heavy weight to bear, and it should not be grievous to give it. God is not trying to *take* something from you, but rather, He is trying to *get* something to you. We are to believe and understand the benefit of the tithe and rejoice in it. The tithe is an act of worship that declares that God is our source. It has well-defined benefits that, when we tithe, we should be in faith to receive.

I always suggest a family already have their tithe made out when they come to church. I also suggest that, before they come to church, they lay their hands on that tithe, declare the benefit of it, and declare that the windows of heaven are open and that Satan is rebuked off of their harvest. They should also declare that Satan cannot steal from them and what they put their hands to will prosper, in the name of Jesus.

Now, lastly, let me wrap up our discussion of the tithe with a look at the tithe as recorded in the New Testament. Oh, yes, the tithe is mentioned there! The following passage is where we read from earlier.

> After Abram returned from defeating Kedorlaomer and the kings allied with him, the king of Sodom came out to meet him in the Valley of Shaveh (that is, the King's Valley). Then Melchizedek king of Salem brought out bread and wine. He was priest of God Most High, and he blessed Abram, saying, "Blessed be Abram by God Most High, Creator of heaven and earth. And praise be to God Most High, who delivered your enemies into your hand." <u>Then Abram gave him a tenth of everything.</u>
>
> —Genesis 14:17–20

Now, let's see what the writer of Hebrews says about the tithe.

> This Melchizedek was king of Salem and priest of God Most High. He met Abraham returning from the defeat of the kings and blessed him, and Abraham gave him a tenth of everything. First, the name Melchizedek means "king of righteousness"; then also, "king of Salem" means "king of peace." Without father or mother, without genealogy, without beginning of days or end of life, resembling the Son of God, he remains a priest forever. Just think how great he was: Even the patriarch Abraham gave him a tenth of the plunder! Now the law requires the descendants of Levi who become priests to collect a tenth from the people—that is, from their fellow Israelites—even though they also are descended from Abraham. This man, however, did not trace his descent from Levi, yet he collected a tenth from Abraham and blessed him who had the promises. And without doubt the lesser is blessed by the greater. In the one case, the

tenth is collected by people who die; but in the other case, by him who is declared to be living.

—Hebrews 7:1–8

Please note that this text says, "*In the one case, the tenth is collected by people who die,*" referring to the Levites of the Old Testament. Then it goes on to say, "*But in the other case, by him **who is declared to be living**.*"

It says Melchizedek was the king of righteousness, king of peace, without mother or father, without beginning of days or end of life, resembling the Son of God, a priest forever. Melchizedek was Jesus Christ standing before Abraham that day. He was not known as Jesus at that moment however.

Remember, Joseph was told by the angel to name the baby boy Jesus when He was born. The name Jesus means Savior, thus indicating by His name who He was to be to us. Christ is not Jesus's last name. When we say Jesus Christ, we are literally saying the anointed Savior. Jesus was not known by the name Jesus when He stood before Abraham, because that plan was still being hidden from Satan at that time.

So, the name Melchizedek was a name that simply reflected who He was, the King of Righteousness and the Prince of Peace. However, prophetically, Melchizedek was declaring Abraham's future by serving him bread and wine, which spoke of the new covenant (bread, His body broken for us, and the wine, His blood given for us) that would be made with the heirs of Abraham later on and would fulfill the promise that God gave to Abraham regarding his heirs in Genesis 12.

In regard to the tithe, Hebrews says the tithe is now collected by "him who is declared to be living." It is Jesus who now collects the tithe, the one who is declared to be living! He is the King of kings and the Lord of lords.

So, remember, the law of the tithe is still in effect today. The only thing that has changed is the priesthood. In the Old Testament, the tribe of Levi collected the tithe for the work of God. Today, Jesus (who came from the tribe of Judah, not Levi, indicating a new order of the priesthood was established) collects the tithe from His church for the work of the ministry. Of course, I realize that Jesus, the person, is not here personally collecting the tithe. But remember that the Bible says the church is the body of Christ, meaning His legal expression here, just as our body gives us legal expression here. As we give to His church, His body, we are in fact giving to Jesus. The Levites, under the old covenant, collected the tithe on behalf of God's ministry then, and the church collects the tithe on behalf of God's ministry now.

In review, the tithe is a legal fence around your life that stops the devil from having access to steal your provision. Remember, the tithe by itself does not cause you to prosper! Your prosperity is determined by what you do *inside* that fence!

The tithe is a law that is vital to your financial life. This is why I took so much time covering this important law of the Kingdom.

So, the next time you are at church and the pastor says it is time to receive the tithes, you should shout for joy, because now you know the benefits of the tithe.

ABOUT THE AUTHOR

Gary Keesee is a television host, author, international speaker, financial expert, successful entrepreneur, and pastor who has made it his mission to help people win in life, especially in the areas of faith, family, and finances.

After years of living in poverty, Gary and his wife, Drenda, discovered the principles of the Kingdom of God, and their lives were drastically changed. Together, under the direction of the Holy Spirit, they created several successful businesses and paid off all of their debt. Now, they spend their time declaring the Good News of the Kingdom of God around the world through Faith Life Now, their organization that exists to motivate, educate, and inspire people from all walks of life and backgrounds to pursue success, walk out their God-designed purposes, and leave positive spiritual and moral legacies for their families.

Faith Life Now produces two television programs—*Fixing the Money Thing* and *Drenda*—as well as practical resources, conferences, and speaking events around the world.

Gary is also the president and founder of Forward Financial Group and the founding pastor of Faith Life Church, which has campuses in New Albany and Powell, Ohio.

Gary and Drenda, their five adult children and their spouses, and their grandchildren all reside in Central Ohio.

For additional resources by both Gary and Drenda, visit FaithLifeNow.com.

FINANCIAL REVOLUTION CONFERENCES

If you're a pastor or leader in your church, you probably have plenty of vision for your ministry. But do you have the money or resources you need to support the vision?

If your church is like most churches, the answer is probably *not quite* or even *no*.

Why?

We've found one of the biggest reasons is DEBT. So many Christians are being held *hostage* by debt.

Your people *WANT* to financially support the ministry and vision of your church, but many of them are living paycheck to paycheck with no hope of breaking free.

We can help.

For more than 25 years now, we've been working with churches of all sizes, helping them reach their goals and see their visions for their ministries become reality. And the best part is that this is completely free!

We help churches by helping their people. We can help *your church* by helping *your people*.

Learn more at **ftmtevent.com.**

OCCUPY YOUR DESTINY

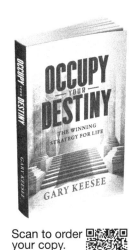

Scan to order your copy.

You are here *right now* for a purpose—to occupy the unique territory that God has designated for you in this world. And as a believer, Jesus instructed you to do just that—to…

OCCUPY until He comes.

Are you ready to take possession of and secure ALL God has for YOU?

Get positioned to OCCUPY and release the Kingdom of God into the earth until Jesus returns with this perspective-changing and profoundly impactful book by Gary Keesee!

Gary Keesee knows firsthand what it takes to succeed against all odds and wants to show YOU how to discover your destiny, occupy the territory created just for you, and WIN in life.

In his down-to-earth, practical, and easily-applied style, Gary shares biblical truths and direction with unique revelation that applies to your everyday life, showing you how to discover your destiny and occupy until Jesus comes.

God has so much more for you. It's time to OCCUPY all He has for you!

Don't wait. Get your copy of *Occupy Your Destiny: The Winning Strategy for Life* TODAY at garykeesee.com.

> *"This book is about YOU and your destiny—not just getting you there but showing you how to OCCUPY that place once you're there. This is something most people have never been taught."*

—Gary Keesee

UNFINISHED BUSINESS

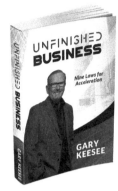

Scan to order your copy.

More than 80% of Americans don't like their jobs.

Are *you* one of them?

Are you staying somewhere you don't want to be just to pay your bills?

Have financial issues or debt hijacked your freedom and forced you to give up on your dreams?

It's time for a change!

Don't allow God's plan for YOUR life to go unfinished!

Discover the simple steps you can take to change your mindset, see and SEIZE the opportunities all around you, accelerate your success, and reach your dreams!

Don't wait. Get your copy of *Unfinished Business: The Nine Laws of Acceleration* today at garykeesee.com!

> *"There are NINE Kingdom laws the Lord revealed to me that you need to know to accelerate into the destiny He has for you and finish your assignment!"*

—Gary Keesee

YOUR FINANCIAL REVOLUTION 5-BOOK PAPERBACK BOXED SET

Scan to order your copy.

→

Gary Keesee went from being completely desperate financially and physically to healthy and whole, paying cash for cars, building his home free from debt, starting multiple companies, and teaching hundreds of thousands of people about Kingdom living each week through television, ministry, and books just like these.

What changed for Gary, and how can it change YOUR LIFE?

Your answers are in the pages of THIS book series.

This isn't just another set of books with tips on how to fix your finances.

Full of fresh revelation, powerful examples from the Word of God, and inspiring personal stories about Gary and others who applied the foundational teachings from these five Kingdom principles in their own lives and experienced drastic change as a result, this series of books was written to help YOU experience real change in EVERY area of your life.

No matter your situation, there are answers. It's never too late.

You can have your own amazing story!

Join Gary Keesee on this incredible five-part journey of discovery that will completely revolutionize YOUR life… just like it did his.

This set contains paperback versions of Gary's complete *Your Financial Revolution* book series:

- *Your Financial Revolution: The Power of Allegiance*
- *Your Financial Revolution: The Power of Rest*
- *Your Financial Revolution: The Power of Strategy*
- *Your Financial Revolution: The Power of Provision*
- *Your Financial Revolution: The Power of Generosity*

Get your copy of the complete *Your Financial Revolution* five-book series at garykeesee.com.